Leonard Griffith

We
Have
This
Ministry

WORD BOOKS, *Publisher, Waco, Texas*

Preface

In May 1972 Dr. Leonard Griffith presented the messages that are being published in this book as the Raney Lectures in Little Rock, Arkansas.

The T. J. and Inez Raney Lectureship was established in 1951 by Mr. and Mrs. Alton B. Raney, Mrs. Dallas P. Raney and the late Dallas P. Raney, and Mr. and Mrs. Robert W. Raney, Mr. and Mrs. Tom Raney, and Mr. and Mrs. Clay Raney in memory of Mr. and Mrs. T. J. Raney, consecrated leaders in Arkansas Methodism. The lectures have been given annually in the sanctuary of Pulaski Heights United Methodist Church. The lectureship was the first of its kind to be established in Arkansas, and it has served as a model for more than twenty similar lectureships in various communities within the state.

The purpose of the lectureship is to bring to Little Rock, and to Arkansas, distinguished ministers who will enrich the spiritual life of the community and the state.

The Raney Lectures have become a vital event in the lives of Christians of all denominations who eagerly anticipate the series from year to year. This place has been achieved wholly as a result of distinguished ministers who have been participants since the series' inception. These include: Dr. Roy L. Smith, Bishop Paul E. Martin, Dr. Ralph Sockman, Dr. Marshall T. Steel, Dr. George Buttrick, Dr. Charles Ray Goff, Dr. Elton Trueblood, Dr. Paul Scherer, Dr. Louis H. Evans, Dr. Robert J. McCracken, Bishop Richard C. Raines, Dr. J. Kenneth Shamblin, Dr. Charles L. Allen, Bishop Gerald Kennedy, and Dr. Bryant M. Kirkland.

Dr. Griffith's profoundly relevant messages and his warm personality captivated all who came to hear him. I hope that this volume will give these lectures the widespread exposure they so compellingly deserve.

JAMES B. ARGUE
Senior Minister
Pulaski Heights United Methodist Church
Little Rock, Arkansas

*"Therefore seeing we have this ministry,
as we have received mercy, we faint not."*
2 Corinthians 4:1, KJV

Contents

*"Men and women who expect to share Christ's ministry . . .
must understand that its . . . main motive . . .
is to bring God into the experience of men
and to bring men into the presence of God."*

BETWEEN GOD AND MAN

Chapter 1

We have this ministry . . .

Between God and Man

The Pattern Ministry

ROBERT FLYNN'S novel, *In the House of the Lord*,[1] creates a Protestant minister with the un-Protestant name of Pat Shahan and tells the story of what is supposed to be a typical day in his ministry.

Some day! People start knocking on his vestry door before he has time to take off his coat. First comes a young Sunday school teacher, wrongly accused of homosexual conduct, who decides that he had better transfer to another church. Next comes the treasurer who argues that a few hundred dollars might be saved by spreading a cheaper

1. Alfred A. Knopf, New York, 1969.

fertilizer on the church lawn. (That could be symbolic!) There are telephone arguments—with a social worker about the distribution of Thanksgiving baskets, and with a newspaper reporter about the church's intention to admit a Negro into membership. Next comes an interview with a middle-aged spinster who plays her scratchy gramophone record of how she stayed at home and cared for her father and how her father died and left the house to her married sisters. Pat advises her to forgive her sisters. He goes to lunch with a candidate for political office who is worried because his hydroelectric company cut off the power in some nonpaying homes and caused the death of a boy in an iron lung.

After lunch Pat rushes to the hospital where he stands beside a woman who keeps vigil at her husband's deathbed. Back at the church he interviews an oversexed girl who wants to talk about theology but is interested more in his body than in his mind. He blunders his way through a counseling session with an engaged couple who ought not to be getting married in the church or anywhere else. He goes to console a widow whose husband committed suicide by crashing his airplane in a stunt at an evangelistic crusade. One of the sisters of the middle-aged spinster whom he advised that morning gives him hell on the telephone, but that's mild compared to what he gets from a mousy little man whom he tries to talk out of donating his life's savings to provide a revolving cross for the church steeple.

Do you wonder that Pat's nerves are shot by the time he gets home? Do you wonder that he takes it out on his wife and children, hating himself for it? He can think of no greater luxury in the world than to be like most of the men in his neighborhood—to stay at home for the evening with his family, talk to his wife, play with his children, relax by the television set, be a whole person. But no, he has to inhale his dinner and then go to a meeting of the local council of churches. With some sympathy the author writes, "All day long people had come to him with their problems, and he had fought their battles, sought their answers. All day he had fought alone, in an exposed position, outnumbered, without encouragement or support, with no shield except a calloused heart, with no weapon except blame. He had returned at the end of the day weary, used up, defeated. And now he had to go back again" (p. 222).

Poor Pat! He wonders how much longer he can take it. In fact, if someone had told him in seminary that the ministry could be such a drag, such a grind, such a relentless round of human hypocrisy, crippling crises, and petty problems, he would have opted out while there was time and never allowed himself to be ordained.

Why didn't someone tell him in seminary? Why didn't some sensitive professor or some kindly senior minister warn him what to expect if he went ahead with his crazy scheme to be ordained and become the pastor of a busy church? Of course, the story seems somewhat contrived. No minister runs the whole gamut of human crises in twenty-four hours. He may have to deal with all of Pat's problems over a longer period of time; but to crowd them, as the novelist does, into a single day stretches the imagination. Most of us have not found the ministry that demanding or even that interesting.

The author keeps punctuating his narrative with little dialogues, in block capitals, between Pat and God.

" 'ARE YOU A HUMBLE MAN, PAT?' "

" 'No, Lord, but I'd be proud to be one.' "

I wish the story had included a dialogue between Pat and Jesus. I wish the distressed young pastor had heard the voice of Jesus saying, "Stop pitying yourself, Pat.

[15

So you feel beaten, bullied, and whipped by the demands that people make on you, inconsiderate people who are so troubled that they can think of no one but themselves. Well, that's what you bargained for when you entered my ministry. And it *is* *my* ministry. Read about it in the Gospels. They tell you about a typical day in my earthly career, a day that begins, continues, and ends with crises, a day of involvement in human need, battling with human hypocrisy, a day that leaves me depleted, exhausted, and ready to quit—except that I find renewal in prayer. So why should it be any different for you, Pat? A servant is not greater than his Lord."

A course that I should like to see included in the seminary curriculum is a depth study of the ministry of Jesus in the Gospels. There would be no tricky exegesis, no academic credits, no examinations, and maybe no teacher. It would be informal but compulsory, a serious seminar in which men and women who intend to serve the Church in any capacity would try to get alongside the historic Jesus and make up their minds what he came to do, how he went about it, what were his priorities, how people reacted to him, how he reacted to them, how he dealt with their needs and problems, how he handled his own successes and failures. There might be fewer ordinands after such a course, but those who stick would at least be ordained with their eyes open. Studying the ministry of Jesus in the Gospels, they would see it as a pattern of their own ministry and say with truth, "It's going to be exactly like that."

We are not all preachers or seminarians, but if we are servants of Christ we are the people whom Paul had in mind when he wrote, "*Therefore, seeing we have this ministry, as we have received mercy, we faint not*" (2 Cor. 4:1, KJV). By "this ministry," Paul meant Christ's ministry which he began during his earthly career, which he continues through his living presence, and which he commits to all his followers. Paul believed that every community of Christians, whatever its size and structure, its methods and techniques, exists for no other reason than to share and continue the gospel ministry of Christ. In the following chapters we shall explore some of the most obvious features of that ministry, not only for their own sake but also as a pattern of the kind of ministry which the whole Church and our churches in particular are called to exercise.

THE PENDULUM-PRINCIPLE

When we do look closely at the gospel ministry of Jesus we are astonished at how much of it was spent doing absolutely nothing. Jesus prayed a great deal; and in the minds of some people that amounts to doing absolutely nothing. The telephone rings in the church office, and a voice says, "I would like to speak to the pastor. Is he busy?" The answer comes back, "No, he's not busy. He's in the chapel praying."

Jesus had his private chapel to which he constantly withdrew for prayer. It might be the wilderness or a desert place or a mountaintop or a fishing boat on the Sea of Galilee. Sometimes he withdrew alone, sometimes he took with him a few intimate friends, sometimes he took the twelve disciples. He spent a night in that chapel before choosing the twelve disciples (Luke 6:12–16). He withdrew there before every great decision and at the height of every crisis. His whole ministry had a rhythm to it like the rhythm of sleeping and waking, rest and work, a constant pattern of withdrawal and return. Every encounter with men was balanced by an encounter with God, and

[17

every period spent with God was followed by a period of involvement in the affairs of men. Like the swing of a pendulum his ministry moved back and forth between prayer and service, between direct communication with God and direct communication with men.

In view of the brevity of Jesus' earthly career, probably a period of eighteen months, and in view of its hectic busyness, "no leisure even to eat" (Mark 6:31), is it not astonishing that he found so much time to be alone with God? No, not astonishing when you consider what he came on earth to do. Even if he had come only to help people, to cure their diseases and straighten their twisted limbs and teach them lessons about God, he would still have prayed regularly and frequently. His ministry exhausted him at times; he needed to pray in order to replenish his strength, re-create his energies, renew his enthusiasm, and restore his perspective.

But Jesus came to do more than help people in a practical way. He came to do what no one else could do for them. He came to reconcile them to God. This was the main motive of his ministry—to bring God into the experience of men and to bring men into the presence of God. Before all else Jesus was to be a mediator between God and man, a priest who represented God to man and man to God. Therefore he was *not* doing absolutely nothing when he withdrew to pray; he was performing an essential half of his ministry. Jesus *had* to maintain a rhythm of withdrawal and return. He *had* to strike a balance between prayer and service. He *had* to spend as much time with God as he spent with man.

Look now at four series of incidents from the Gospel story which illustrate the pendulum-principle in Jesus' life. Begin with Mark's account of the Galilean ministry (1:14–45). On the Sabbath day Jesus withdraws to the synagogue at Capernaum. Having worshiped God, he teaches "with authority" and heals an insane man who recognizes him as "the Holy One of God." Then he goes to Simon's house where he cures that disciple's mother-in-law of a fever. After sunset the house becomes like the outpatients' department of a hospital, as people from all over the city bring their sufferers and lay them at the feet of the Great Physician. Sleep alone does not restore his depleted energy and equip him for another such demanding day. He must withdraw again to spend time with God. We find him next morning before dawn praying by himself in a lonely place. The disciples soon interrupt his privacy. "Every one is searching for you," they tell him; and Jesus goes with them because he now has God's power for everyone, for a leper whom he cleanses of the loathsome disease and for a paralyzed man whom he heals by forgiving his sins.

Look at the events in Matthew's Gospel (14:13-33) which surround the feeding of the five thousand. Shocked by the news that John the Baptist had been capriciously put to death, Jesus withdrew to a lonely place on the shore of the Sea of Galilee. The crowds soon caught up with him, and he taught them and healed the sick because he had compassion. Sensing the signs of hunger among the people, he told his disciples to look for food. All they could muster were five loaves and two fish—a little boy's lunch. "Bring them here to me," Jesus said. Taking them in his hands, he withdrew for a moment, spiritually, then he distributed those meager rations among several thousand people and satisfied their physical hunger. Dismissing everybody, he went up into the hills to pray alone. Meanwhile, his disciples set out across the lake in their fishing boat. They were about halfway when a sudden storm arose and threw them into panic. Suddenly they saw what

[19

looked like a ghost walking on the water beside them. It was Jesus. He spoke to them, saying, "Take heart, it is I; have no fear." Peter, who must have had a strong faith or illusions of divinity, leaped impulsively into the water, thinking it would hold him up also. He might have drowned, had not the strong arm of Jesus drawn him to safety. When the storm ceased, and they reached land, the awe-stricken disciples worshiped Jesus, saying, "Truly you are the Son of God."

Look at the transfiguration story (Mark 9:2–29) which is recorded in three of the Gospels. On that occasion Jesus deliberately left a great crowd of needy people in the valley while he and three of his disciples went up a high mountain to pray. On the summit the disciples saw their Master drenched in dazzling light, flanked by Moses and Elijah, and they heard a voice that came from a cloud, saying, "This is my beloved Son; listen to him." Peter decided that Jesus ought to stay there—but that would have been a mistake. It would also have been a mistake if Jesus had never come there, because he received power through his conversation with God. Possessed of that power, he went back to the valley where he found a mob surrounding a distraught father with a drooling, groaning, convulsing epileptic child. Nearby stood the religious leaders arguing helplessly about the situation. The disciples were equally helpless. After Jesus had cured the lad and given him back to his father, they asked why they couldn't cast out the demon. Jesus replied, "This kind cannot be driven out by anything but prayer."

Look at the events of the last twelve hours of Jesus' earthly life. The drama begins in the Upper Room where he institutes the Last Supper and offers to God a long sustained prayer for his disciples and for all who will believe in him through their word (John 17:1–26). Waiting to be arrested in the Garden of Gethsemane, Jesus leaves his disciples while he withdraws to wrestle with God in prayer (Matt. 26:36–46). Having surrendered to the will of God, he goes out empowered to do the greatest thing that God has ever done for men.

Prayer seems to be the dominant feature of his final tragic hours. Three of his seven utterances from the cross are prayers (Luke 23:34, 43, 46). He intercedes for his crucifiers, "Father, forgive them, for they know not what they do." A pendulum swings back and he gives the penitent thief, hanging beside him, a promise beyond all deserving, "Today you will be with me in Paradise." Even his dying breath is a prayer: "Father, into thy hands I commit my spirit," and it so shakes the soul of his Roman executioner, that this hardened soldier, admitting the innocence of his victim, falls on his knees before God.

So it is no mystery why the seminary curriculum should include a depth study of the ministry of Jesus in the Gospels. Men and women who expect to share Christ's ministry—and surely they have no other valid reason for being ordained—must understand that its purpose is not simply to make people more human but to make them more godlike. They must understand that the main motive of Christ's ministry, whatever form it takes, is to bring God into the experience of men and to bring men into the presence of God. That means that they are not doing absolutely nothing when they pray. On the contrary, they are continuing the priestly ministry of Christ, representing men because they spend time with men, representing God because they spend time with God. The minister is not only a man for others; he is a man for God. He has a duty to serve and a duty to pray; and he must strike a balance between the two, or his ministry will be lopsided and unfruitful. Alexander Stalker expressed it concisely when

[21

he said, "No one has the power of God with men unless he has power with God for men."

WHERE THE ACTION IS NOT

What it all means for the Church was dramatized negatively by a television play called "Reddick" presented a few years ago by the Canadian Broadcasting Corporation. It was a predictable story of a gifted young minister serving an inner-city church, a dying cause kept artificially alive by a handful of stubborn members living a long distance away. They didn't really approve of Reddick's ministry to the hippies and motorcycle gangs in the immediate neighborhood, but they tolerated it as long as he confined it to the church basement. That suited the young people. Only the basement interested them anyway. They furnished it like a discotheque and called it the "Well Hole" and came there in the evenings to listen to rock music. They were willing to use the church basement.

When some of the young people found out that Reddick was being wooed by an affluent church in the suburbs, without waiting to hear that he had turned it down, they put him on trial before an accusation meeting, charging him with exploiting their situation to promote his own career. As evidence they cited excerpts from his private diary which they had stolen and copied. The trial moved upstairs to the sanctuary where Reddick was imprisoned in the pulpit while an inquisitor shouted at him phrases from the Apostles' Creed, each time demanding, "Is that literally true? Do you believe it?"

In the riot that ensued, one of them tossed a big Bible on the communion table, smashing the glasses and spilling the unfermented wine (it was the Canadian counterpart of a Methodist Church). Another began waving a knife and, when he plunged it downward, accidentally thrust it through Reddick's hand.

Many viewers applauded the play enthusiastically. They saw it not only as an authentic portrayal of the modern ministry but as a picture of what the Church ought to be doing in the world today—getting alongside rebellious youth, listening to them, being judged by them, helping them on their own terms, even suffering at their hands. A book published by the United Church of Canada told the story of several such experiments in Canadian cities, some of which have gone defunct since the book was written. The author entitled it, *The Church Is Where the Action Is*, implying that the center of Christian gravity has shifted and that the real Church is precisely not in the sanctuary but in the basement. After all, wasn't that the pattern of Christ's ministry? He didn't waste time worshiping with members of the Establishment in the antiseptic environment of the temple courts. He went down into the basements of life where he found the young toughs, the disestablished members of society, and identified himself with them in their need.

My own reaction to "Reddick" was less wildly enthusiastic. I saw those young toughs, putting their minister on trial, as caricatures of Christians who relate themselves to the secular side of Christ's ministry but not to its spiritual side, forgetting or not even knowing that the pendulum swings in both directions. To me they illustrated the weakness of basement religion. Because they didn't normally go up into the sanctuary, they argued about its faith with the same degree of ignorance that they might have displayed arguing about physics in a science laboratory. Because they cut themselves off from those who worshiped in the sanctuary Sunday after Sunday, they had no sense of community in the whole people of God, no sense of involvement in the total mission of the Church. Because they lacked the humility of people before God, they censured the Church by their standards, not God's; they judged the Word of God rather than allowing it to judge them. They typified the lopsided religion of many people today whose Christianity is related to the basement but not to the sanctuary, whose lives are oriented to men but not to God.

It is obvious from reading the New Testament that the Church, if it consciously continues the ministry of Christ, will want to be where the action is; it will shelter the homeless, feed the hungry, heal the sick, perform a ministry of practical service. Yet it is equally obvious that the Church, if it consciously continues the ministry of Christ, will be where the action is not; it will perform a ministry of prayer and worship. Many secular agencies today are performing ministries of service and performing them expertly and strategically, but which of the secular agencies performs a ministry of prayer? Which of them brings God into human experience? Which reconciles men to God? Only the Church performs that priestly role. The Church that patterns its purpose on the purpose of Christ will recognize that it exists not only to *do* something but to *be* something. It must be to the world what Christ was to the world—a priest, a mediator, a meeting place between God and man. That means that just as there was a rhythm, a pendulum-swing of withdrawal and return in Christ's ministry, so there must be the same rhythm, the same pendulum-swing of withdrawal and return in the Church's ministry. We have a duty to serve and a duty to pray, and we cannot neglect either duty if we want to be faithful ministers of Christ.

There are times when the greatest thing that the Church can do for the world is to pray for it. John Henry Jowett used to tell of a servant girl in his congregation who had a deep concern for her calling as a Christian. When he asked her how she proposed to live the Christian life, she answered, "I haven't much time left from my work, sir, and I can't attend meetings at the church or even many services." "What do you do?" Jowett asked her. "Well, sir," she replied, "I always take the newspaper to bed with me at night." Jowett was puzzled. "What's the good of that?" "Well, sir, I read the birth notices and I pray for the babies that have been born. I read the deaths and I pray that God's comfort may come to these sorrowing homes."

That humble servant girl could be a figure of the Church engaged in the mediating ministry of Christ. Maybe it isn't always possible for the Church to be where the action is. Governments, universities, labor unions, social agencies, the press, radio, and television have become the institutions of great power and influence today. To a large extent they have taken over the Church's role and reduced the Church to servant status in a secular society that sometimes scorns the Church and refuses to accept its service.

Yet the Church can still play its own distinctively important role where the action is not—Christ's role of a priest and mediator between God and man. The Church fulfills that role in the sanctuary. When we come to the sanctuary we are all priests. We represent the world before God, we acknowledge God as its Creator and Ruler, we confess the sins of the world and ask God's forgiveness, we voice the perplexities of the world and seek his guidance, we speak for the needs of the world and implore his help. Then we go back into the world to represent God before a secular society, to bring God into human experience, to reconcile men to God.

We can be sure that if we don't do it, nobody else will. As servants of Jesus Christ, "we have *this* ministry."

[25

*". . . if the Church concentrated less on the rescue operation
and more on the persons it ought to be rescuing,
then the Church would have the priorities of Jesus,
and people might respond to the Church again
as they responded to Jesus."*

PUTTING PERSONS FIRST

Chapter 2

We have this ministry . . .

Putting Persons First

THE WORLD'S PRIORITIES

SUPPOSE that a doctor working in his laboratory and hospital ward discovers a cure for cancer. What indescribable good news! The sentence of death lifted from so many lives! Having been discovered, the cure is permanently there but it is not yet available to cancer sufferers all over the world. A corps of doctors must learn about it and be taught how to handle it; they must become the agents whereby the cure becomes universally available.

That is a figure of the continuing ministry of Jesus. Here on earth, at a place which can be located and a date which can be fixed, Jesus gave the human race its only cure to the deadly disease of sin. "It is accomplished!" he cried from his cross (John 19:30, NEB). The cure is permanently there—that is the good news—but it cannot be made available to sinners all over the world unless a corps of Christians learns about it and goes out to administer it. That is the Church's role in history. *"We have this ministry,"* Paul wrote in his second letter to the Corinthians (4:1, KJV); and Paul means Christ's ministry which he accomplished in the days of his flesh and which he committed to all who profess his name. Our supreme role, as preachers or laymen, as members of local congregations and of the whole Church throughout the world, is to study the gospel ministry of Jesus, to learn about it and make it universally available.

We continue our study by looking at an event reported in three of the Gospels. Early one morning Jesus restored sanity to an insane man who had been cast out of normal society and forced to find his asylum among the tombs of the dead. The man believed that he was possessed by a thousand demons; so Jesus, in order to cure him, had to show him that the demons had left his body and found another dwelling place. He sent them, or sent something, into a nearby herd of pigs, causing them to stampede and rush headlong over a steep cliff into the Sea of Galilee. The local farmers weren't very happy about all that floating pork. They didn't begrudge the healing miracle—they were not inhuman—but they couldn't see why it had to happen at the expense of their livestock. The Gospel says that "they began to beg Jesus to depart from their neighborhood" (Mark 5:17)—which puts it rather mildly. They probably said, "You care for men; we care for swine. That's where we differ, so get out!"

You can see the contrast in values. The farmers put pigs first, people second. Jesus put people first, pigs second. People were his priority. One of the first things we have to do, when we study the Master's ministry as a pattern for the Church's ministry, is to decide on the basis of the Gospels what are its priorities. That is especially important when we realize that the Church today lives in a society which is terribly mixed up in its priorities.

Here is an example not unlike the incident of the demoniac. It concerns a television documentary which presented a report about starvation among children in Latin America. The commentator said that they had food to eat but not enough food with the right nutritional strength. After the commentary came the commercial— an advertisement for a high-cost, especially nutritious dog food. The switch called for some adjustment in the mind of the viewer. After looking at thin fibrous beans and crumbly bread in cracked bowls, he now had to look at a close-up of red meaty chunks covered with thick gravy. It left the viewer not only with the shocking awareness that his shaggy terrier was eating better than millions of people in the same hemisphere but with the uneasy feeling that the media, the advertisers, society, and he himself cared more about the terrier than about the hungry people.[1]

Another glaring example of mixed up priorities can be seen in the prestigious point of view that puts the space race ahead of the human race. After space experts, having landed men on the moon, began planning expeditions to Mars at an astronomical cost, the *Christian Century* in an editorial pleaded for "a radical reorientation of values." It declared, "Let us say No to Mars until we have said Yes to men, women and children for whom the quality of life and even existence itself are cruelly shut off." [2]

1. Told by William Kuhns in *Environmental Man* (New York: Harper & Row Publishers, 1969), p. 104.
2. June 11, 1969.

[31

When the Southern Christian Leadership Conference staged a protest march at Cape Kennedy, the director, Hosea Williams, said, "We are not against things like the space shot. But there's been a miscalculation in priorities. If the Government can spend the kind of money it has to keep a man alive in space, then why can't it spend enough to keep a man alive here on earth?"

But why pick on the space program? Are not the expenditures or projected expenditures on sports stadiums and the fabulous salaries paid to professional athletes and entertainers sinfully ludicrous as long as two-thirds of the earth's population go to bed hungry every night? In 1960 Elvis Presley was paid $125,000 for one night's appearance on a TV program. He did two wriggles and sang two songs, and for this received more than the yearly salary of the president of the United States. At the time it was estimated that an identical sum of money would pay the annual salaries of 25 school teachers, 42 ministers or 63 farmhands. It would provide a year's training for 30 or more nurses, would give 125 young people a year in college, would stock 10 mission hospitals with elemental tools and drugs, would feed 3000 refugee children for a whole year.

Our society is all mixed up in its priorities, and it is the Church's business to straighten them out—unless the Church also happens to be mixed up; in which case the Church needs to take a closer look at the priorities of Jesus.

THE PRIORITIES OF JESUS

Every person has his own priorities. You can usually tell what they are by asking three questions about him: (1) What does he have time for? (2) How does he spend his wealth? (3) What does he allow to interrupt him?

When we ask those questions about Jesus, the Gospels give an immediate answer. What did he have time for? Persons. He led the busiest of lives, he had "no leisure even to eat," he moved with a sense of urgency because he knew that his time was rapidly running out; yet he always found time for persons, time to chat with a man at midnight or a woman at midday, time to visit the home of friends or to take little children upon his knee.

How did he spend his wealth, which was not money but the power of God? On persons. If you read the Gospels carefully you will see that, whenever they describe Jesus as being particularly conscious of Divine power, they immediately tell how he used that power for some act of service to men. The most dramatic example is his washing of the disciples' feet (John 13:3–5).

What did Jesus allow to interrupt him? Persons. It didn't matter what he was doing—preaching a sermon, eating a meal, taking his rest, praying—he could always be interrupted by persons who needed him. Persons were his priority. He put persons first.

We have already seen that Jesus put persons before things—and that included all things, animal, vegetable, and mineral. "You care for men; we care for swine," declared the irate farmers after Jesus had healed the demoniac. They were right. Jesus did care for men. That was the motive behind his frontal attack on the laws governing Sabbath observance. He didn't want to undermine those laws but he did want to expose their distortion of people's priorities and he wanted to straighten them out. "The sabbath was made for man, not man for the sabbath" (Mark 2:27), he told the Pharisees. When they objected to his acts of healing on the Sabbath Day, he called them hypocrites and accused them of being kinder to their

[33

donkeys and sheep and oxen than they were to people (Luke 13:15). Again he said, "What man of you, if he has one sheep and it falls into a pit on the sabbath, will not lay hold of it and lift it out? Of how much more value is a man than a sheep!" (Matt. 12:11–12).

Jesus put persons before institutions. Here again his priorities contrasted sharply with those of his contemporaries. One day, as he stood with his disciples in the temple at Jerusalem, they said to him, "Look, Teacher, what wonderful stones and what wonderful buildings!" (Mark 13:1). It was the normal reaction of country boys to the big buildings of the great city. A moment earlier Jesus also had said "Look!" but he was not pointing to the temple. He was pointing to a poor widow who had dropped two copper coins, her total wealth, into the temple treasury (Mark 12:41–44). In his eyes that was the big thing, the really wonderful thing, the mightiest financial transaction in the world. Precisely because the temple buildings represented an institution that did not notice persons like the poor widow, precisely because they exploited such persons rather than serving them, Jesus predicted their destruction. "There will not be left here one stone upon another, that will not be thrown down" (13:2).

Jesus put persons before people. He was always stopping to help them, always turning his attention from the many to the one. He said that the whole world could not be set in the balance over against one human soul (Mark 8:36). He said that all heaven's energies are sometimes directed to the salvation of one lost soul (Luke 15:1–10).

In Capernaum one day he was preaching to a large congregation when a distraught father interrupted the sermon and begged him to come and heal his sick daughter. Jesus, valuing persons more highly than congregations, stopped preaching and "went with him" (Mark 5:24).

In Jericho, where the people lined the streets to get a sight of him, Jesus heard the cries of a blind beggar above the shouts of the crowd and for the sake of that one lowly individual he stopped and said, "Call him" (Mark 10:49).

In Bethany, where his disciples criticized a woman for an extravagant gesture toward him, saying that the money should have been given to the poor, Jesus rebuked them, not because he didn't care for the poor but because he cared for that particular poor person whose extravagance met her own deepest need (Matt. 26:6–13).

Jesus put persons even before the success of his own mission. That's what took him to the cross. He was safe as long as he simply preached sermons and taught disciples and proclaimed broad, general principles about God and man and love and the Kingdom. Nobody quarrels with preachers and social radicals; they come and they go. It was when Jesus got down to specific cases that his enemies started to worry and began plotting to do away with him. They did not object to his gospel of God's forgiveness; they objected vehemently when he cured a paralyzed man by saying, "My son, your sins are forgiven" (Mark 2:5–7). They were not disturbed by his teaching about life after death; they were dreadfully disturbed when he demonstrated his power by raising Lazarus from the dead (John 11:38–44). Jesus jeopardized his mission for the sake of persons. His care for them took him to Calvary, and even there he went on caring for them to the very end.

CHRISTIAN PRIORITIES

What of the Church's ministry when it is consciously patterned on the ministry of Jesus in the Gospels? Right away its priorities become clear. First and foremost it must be a ministry to persons—not populations, social structures,

[35

cultures, or institutions, but persons. Persons must have first claim upon us, and all else must be subordinate to them. What does that mean for the pastor, the layman, the local congregation and the whole Church? Perhaps we can answer that question in each case by paraphrasing Jesus' words about Sabbath observance: "The sabbath was made for man, not man for the sabbath."

1. To *the ordained minister* we say, "Your career was made for persons, not persons for your career." We can light up these truths with some illustrations from literature. William Golding's novel *The Spire* tells the story of a cathedral in medieval England and the building of a 400-foot spire. This spire becomes not only the brainchild but the obsession of Jocelyn, the Dean. In spite of warnings from experts that the foundations are insecure and the project unsafe, he declares that the spire will rise and the project succeed. It does succeed, much to everyone's surprise. In the end it stands erect like a giant finger pointed to heaven, but it has a hellish shape in the sight of God because it is reared on human sacrifice. It has devoured everything—the master-builder, his wife, some of the workmen, the respect of the parish, even Jocelyn himself. It is raised to the glory of God, yet because of it the service of God has long ceased. It is really not a monument to God at all but a monument to Jocelyn's dubious career.

Every ordained minister knows how easily that spire could become the sad symbol of his career. Endowed with the ambitions of the natural man, he wants to succeed in his profession just as architects, politicians, and lawyers want to succeed in their professions. He wants his career to rise to the heights of personal achievement. But that exposes him to the subtle temptation to treat people not as persons but as materials, as human bodies that make up adoring congregations, as members of committees which he manipulates, as sources of the revenue that pays his salary, as stones that build up his personal spire. Not many ministers succumb totally to the temptation, but most of us recognize it as an ever-present danger. The greatest single problem that ministers face is the problem of priorities, not only in the allotment of time and energy to specific tasks but in the allotment of life itself. We need to soak our souls in the priorities of Jesus and be reminded constantly that persons come first. Our careers are made for persons, not persons for our careers.

2. To *the layman* it could be said that Christian principles are made for persons, not persons for principles. That applies to all relationships, especially the home, which is the most strategic sphere of the layman's ministry. Thorvald Helmer, the male lead in Ibsen's play, *A Doll's House*, is a man of strict Christian principle. He hates deceit and dishonesty. He cannot countenance any kind of crime, especially forgery. He feels physically ill in the company of criminals. Unknown to him, his wife Nora once forged her father's signature on a bank note. She did it out of love for her husband, because he was seriously ill at the time and needed a long holiday in a warm climate which he could not afford. She has been gradually repaying the loan. When the truth of it comes to light, Helmer, who usually speaks to her endearingly, turns on her with consummate cruelty, calls her a hypocrite, a liar, a criminal, an unfit mother, and accuses her of inheriting her father's lack of principle and of having no religion, no morality, no sense of duty. Helmer upholds his precious principles but he loses Nora, even though he magnanimously forgives her when the threat to his own reputation is removed. Nora hoped for something more wonderful. She hoped that

[37

her husband would share her shame and show her that she mattered to him even more than his high Christian principles.

Boris Pasternak makes one of his characters say, "In the Kingdom of God there are only persons." That doesn't mean that there are no principles. Jesus, who embodied the Kingdom, enunciated plenty of principles, but he made it clear that they exist for the sake of persons. Did he learn that lesson from Joseph, his earthly father, whom the New English Bible describes as "a man of principle" (Matt. 1:19)? He had such high principle that, although he saved his pregnant fiancée from public exposure, he resolved to break the engagement. How could he marry a girl who was bearing another man's child? But Joseph changed his mind. The Bible says that an angel appeared to him in a dream and told him the truth about the Divine origin of Mary's baby. I think what really happened is that Joseph loved Mary in spite of all his doubts and all his high principles. To Joseph persons were more precious than principles, and Mary was the most precious person in his life. The Christian layman needs to be reminded of that.

3. The *local congregation* needs to be reminded that programs are made for persons, not persons for programs. A satirical musical revue staged by some seminary students a few years ago, entitled *Sure As You're Born*, projects us to a period in the undetermined future where there are no local congregations. The Church has ceased to exist except as people meet in one another's homes or in vocational and issue-oriented groups. A wistful character, Willis Whitby, is a member of the Claims Adjustors Christian Council, but as a Christian he would like to meet some people other than Claims Adjustors. He comes to visit the Christian Artists Council whose members first welcome his bourgeois approach to their artistic endeavors. But when

it becomes apparent that he does not understand their art
or even their language, they urge him to go elsewhere and
join some other group. Willis sings mournfully, "Where
can I go and be a Person . . . just a Person?"

Presumably he ought to go to an old-fashioned local
congregation where people of all ages, interests, and occu-
pations do come together as persons. Let him not be put
off by the pessimists who predict the demise of the local
church, just because it seems to have drifted from the
center to the periphery of people's lives and loyalties. The
pessimists have an unfortunate habit of taking as their
norm the artificial age of the 1950s when many people in
their post-World War Two insecurity displayed an ab-
normal interest in religion. Some of us grow quite nostalgic
as we remember that golden era of soaring memberships,
skyrocketing budgets, and buildings that bulged at the
seams. Yet the numbers game we played in that satisfying
decade had an inevitable weakness. It treated people as
less than persons. Sometimes it lost sight of persons and
thereby lost touch with the gospel ministry of Jesus. We
had plenty of programs in those days, but often they were
like the bed of Procrustes. People fitted them or else were
made to fit them. We got our priorities mixed. The nu-
merical recession in many local churches today may not be
a bad thing if it is God's way of straightening out our
priorities and reminding us that programs are made for
persons, not persons for programs.

4. To *the whole Church* of Christ throughout the world
it ought to be said that the gospel itself was made for persons, not persons for the gospel. The last literary illustra-
tion comes from the closing chapter of Mark Twain's
Huckleberry Finn where Huck and his friend, Tom
Sawyer, are hatching a plot to liberate old Jim, a runaway
slave whom Tom's uncle has imprisoned in a cabin. Tom's

[39

imagination runs riot as he makes a long list of all the equipment that they will need for the elaborate rescue operation which will be comparable to some of the great escapes in history and which, he speculates, could take years and years, perhaps even a lifetime to carry through. Meanwhile, what about poor old Jim chained to his bed in the dark lonely cabin, without food and drink? He seems to be forgotten. He is only a prop in the drama. The rescue operation itself has become more important than the person to be rescued.

The gospel is God's great rescue operation. God sent Jesus into the world to seek and to save persons. Jesus sent the Church into the world to seek and to save persons. They are the Church's priority. For many lifetimes the Church has been engaged in this rescue operation, and with each generation it has become bigger, costlier and more elaborate—as you can see by a visit to the Vatican in Rome, the World Council of Churches in Geneva, your denominational headquarters, or even that Gothic structure with its impressive education wing at the corner of Main and Third Streets. But there is a question that needs to be asked about this big, costly, elaborate rescue operation which has reached across so many centuries, the question that an American lady had the colossal cheek to ask one of the guides in Westminster Abbey: "Young man, stop your chattering and tell me. Has anyone been saved here lately?"

Colin Morris, who used to be a Methodist missionary in Zambia, wrote a book called *Include Me Out* [3] that dropped like a bomb on the ecumenical movement. Morris wants to be included out of the union negotiations between his church and other churches, not because he is against them

3. Epworth Press, London, 1968.

but because, as he says, he no longer gives a damn one way or the other. What triggered his retreat into "functional neutrality" and prompted him to write the book was the sight of a dead Zambian lying at his front door. The pathologist said he had died of hunger. In his shrunken stomach were a few leaves and what appeared to be a ball of grass. As Morris reads the New Testament, it seems to him that the Church exists for the sake of that little Zambian. *He* should be the Church's priority. It was for his sake that Jesus came, and it was because Jesus cared for such people that others responded to him. Colin Morris has the idea, and it's not such a crazy idea, that if the Church concentrated less on the rescue operation and more on the person it ought to be rescuing, then the Church would have the priorities of Jesus, and people might respond to the Church again as they once responded to Jesus.

"The world saw greatness as a pyramid where,
the closer a man gets to the peak, the higher his prestige,
the lighter his burden, and the more people he commands to serve him.
Jesus inverted the pyramid, so that the closer a man gets to the peak,
the lower his prestige, the heavier his burden,
and the more people he carries in love."

AS ONE THAT SERVES

Chapter 3

We have this ministry . . .

As One That Serves

THE DIVINE STRATEGY

IN METRO TORONTO, where things have not been going too well with the churches, we paid $100,000 to a firm of professional consultants to tell us what we already know. They worked for two years, and worked some of us off our feet compiling statistics and conducting interviews, and finally came up with the depressing fact that the Church is sick and will die within fifteen years unless we administer the right cure. They pinpointed the principal problem as a lack of credible purpose. They said that many congregations exist for a wrong purpose, and some don't know why they exist at all. They said that there must be a radical reorientation of purpose if the Church hopes to recover lost ground and become credible again to the increasing numbers of people who stand outside its life.

Of course, the secular newspapers, especially those with an antichurch bias, had a field day with those gloomy prognostications. The reporters even got around to interviewing me but they didn't quote me, because my comments made poor copy. I told them that the Church has only one credible purpose for its existence, and that is to share the ministry of Jesus which he began during the days of his flesh and which he continues through his living presence. Looking at that ministry in the Gospels, we have seen it as a mediating ministry that brings God into human experience and brings man into the presence of God. Looking at its priorities we have found it to be concerned primarily with persons and their needs. Now we shall go a step further and look at its strategy.

Jesus worked out that strategy in the wilderness of temptation. In fact, that's what the temptation story is all about (Matt. 4:1–11). After his baptism the Spirit of God drove him into the region of the Dead Sea where he remained in solitude without food and drink for nearly six weeks. There he was visited by the Devil who tempted him at three pressure points in his personality: first, at the point of his physical needs—let him use his Divine power to turn stones into bread; second, at the point of his faith —let him leap from the temple tower and trust God to give him a soft landing; third, at the point of his ambitions —let him control the kingdoms of the world by making a deal with the Devil. On all three counts Jesus told the Devil to go where he belonged.

Maybe there was no Devil, no wilderness. It doesn't matter, because Jesus still had to fight that battle in the wilderness of his own mind. The Spirit that drove him to it was the same Spirit that descended on him in his baptism and designated him as God's "beloved Son" (Matt. 3:17). When Jesus emerged from the waters of the Jordan he knew that he was, in fact, the Son of God, the Old Testament Messiah, and that God had commissioned and empowered him to do all that the prophets had foretold that the Messiah would do. He must change the world, save men from their sins, turn human standards upside down, depose evil and enthrone good, inaugurate the Kingdom of God on earth. How to go about doing it? What strategy should he adopt? Bribe people with bread? Dazzle them with miracles? Force them into God's Kingdom? Those were live possibilities. The Old Testament contained some worldly, political, triumphal images of the Messiah; and Jesus, knowing himself to be the Son of God filled with the power of God, would feel tempted to conform to one or more of those images.

He didn't succumb because he was too much of a realist. He had grown up among ordinary people and he knew what went on in their minds and hearts. They might be impressed by bread and circuses but they wouldn't be changed by them. Radical and lasting change can never be imposed on society from without; it has to grow gradually from within—like a mustard seed that becomes a tall tree, or a tiny bit of yeast that causes a whole loaf to rise (Matt. 13:31–33). Jesus knew that you can never make living things grow with a sledge-hammer, no matter how hard you pound. People will not be bullied into the Kingdom of God. That is the world's strategy and it doesn't work. What should he offer in its place? What must be his strategy?

The Suffering Servant

He announced it openly at the beginning of his public

[47

ministry. In his first sermon, which he appropriately preached at his home synagogue in Nazareth (Luke 4:16–30), he took a text from the Old Testament Book of Isaiah (61:1–2) where the author describes the Messiah not in triumphal terms but in terms of lowly service:

"The Spirit of the Lord is upon me,
because he has anointed me to preach good news to the poor.
He has sent me to proclaim release to the captives
and recovering of sight to the blind,
to set at liberty those who are oppressed,
to proclaim the acceptable year of the Lord."

Then Jesus closed the Bible, looked directly at his congregation and said, "Today this scripture has been fulfilled in your hearing." He was saying, in effect, "Yes, I am the Son of God, the Messiah, but not the kind of Messiah you have been expecting. My strategy is not political or supernatural but supremely human; it is to serve the poor, the prisoners, the blind and the oppressed." That apparently didn't please the pious folk of Nazareth. In fact, they got angry and ran Jesus out of town and tried to push him headlong over a cliff. They were not impressed by a servant-image of the Messiah. Neither was John the Baptist who later sent messengers to ask Jesus, "Are you he who is to come, or shall we look for another?" (Luke 7:20).

Yet that was Jesus' strategy, and he never departed from it. He appeared on the stage of history in the role of a servant, the man for others, who asked nothing for himself—no home, no money, no leisure, no privacy. He had everything to give and he gave it freely. On the hillsides he patiently taught the common people lessons about God and the good life in word pictures that they could understand. In the city streets he found the despised and the downcast and gave them back their dignity as human beings in the sight of God. People brought their sick to him, and he healed them in body and spirit. A publican needing to recover his self-respect, or a beggar needing to recover his sight; a rich man worried about his soul, or a fisherman worried about his luck; a leper crying, "Unclean!" or a woman who had sinned—whoever needed Jesus was not denied him. At times he felt the awful weariness of one who spends himself in service to others but he went on spending himself until it took him to the last full measure of devotion on a cross.

Jesus committed that servant-ministry to his disciples. Once *they* recognized him as God's Messiah, he made it crystal clear that, just as he had come to serve, so they must be willing to serve if they wanted to follow him and share his work. Of course, the idea didn't appeal to them at all, it didn't even make sense, but Jesus dealt with them patiently. When he found them arguing about their personal pecking order in the Kingdom of God he said gently, "If anyone would be first, he must be last of all and servant of all" (Mark 9:35). When Peter and John asked to be appointed the chief ministers of state in God's Kingdom, Jesus told all the disciples that "whoever would be great among you must be your servant, and whoever would be first among you must be slave of all" (Mark 10:43–44).

The world saw greatness as a pyramid where, the closer a man gets to the peak, the higher his prestige, the lighter his burdens, and the more people he commands to serve him. Jesus inverted the pyramid, so that the closer a man gets to the peak, the lower his prestige, the heavier his burden, and the more people he carries in love. He pointed to himself and said, "For the Son of man also came not

[49

to be served but to serve, and to give his life as a ransom for many" (Mark 10:45). *That* is the Kingdom of God, the Christian revolution, the radical reversal of earth's standards, the inauguration of an upside-down world.

Still the disciples didn't get the point. Even in the Upper Room, with the cross only a few hours away, they sulkily refused to perform the common courtesy of washing one another's feet. Apparently they had been arguing again about their relative importance in a more or less worldly kingdom and they were in no mood to cast themselves in the role of slaves. Again Jesus reminded them that a slave is the number one man in God's Kingdom. Again he pointed to himself and said, "I am among you as one who serves" (Luke 22:27). To show what he meant he did what they had neglected to do—he washed everybody's feet. He who came from God and was going to God and was filled with the power of God stooped down and scraped filth from the feet of quarreling men. He the Master cast himself in the role of a slave. Now they *did* get the point and they knew instinctively that he would say, "I have given you an example, that you also should do as I have done to you" (John 13:15). That's what Paul was talking about when he wrote to the Church, "We have this ministry."

THE SERVANT CHURCH

Among the parables of Jesus that exalt service as a condition of entrance to God's Kingdom there is one that really spells out the servant-role of the Church. It is the familiar story of a servant who works all day for a prosperous landowner, plowing the fields, tending the livestock, and performing the routine chores. At nightfall he trudges back to the farmhouse with aching limbs and empty stomach. Does the boss or the boss's wife have a hot meal waiting for him? Does he say to the exhausted laborer, "You've had a long day. You must be tired and hungry. Come in at once and sit down at table"? No indeed! The farmer now expects his hired man to serve as cook and butler. Quite as a matter of course he says, "Prepare supper for me, and gird yourself and serve me, till I eat and drink; and afterward you shall eat and drink." It's not a request but an order, the very job that the servant is hired and paid for. And he doesn't get any thanks for it. He doesn't expect to be thanked. Jesus concludes the parable—and he might be speaking to the Church: "So you also, when you have done all that is commanded you, say, 'We are unworthy servants; we have only done what was our duty'" (Luke 17:7–10). That story tells four things about a servant.

1. *A servant is someone who works in somebody else's house.* If the servant represents the Church, and the house represents the world, it means that the Church ceases to be credible when all its activities take place on its own premises for the sake of its own members. Does the Church sometimes project that incredible image to the man who stands outside its life? If so, we should be able to correct his wrong impression. We can tell him that the strange Gothic building on the street corner, to which people travel a long distance by car on Sunday morning and in which they sit like spectators watching a sacred performance put on by professionals, is not some kind of religious theater. We can tell him, when he sees people arriving in the midweek with badminton racquets under their arms, that the Church is not some sort of religious club. We can tell him that the church stands on the street corner not simply to serve its own members but to serve the world around it.

[51

Shall we convince the outsider, or does he see a truer symbol of the Church in Raphael's famous painting of the Transfiguration? It shows the Lord in glory, lifted from the earth, flanked by Moses and Elijah, with the three chosen disciples prostrate in adoration before him. In the foreground, dark against the perspective of the mountain, we see the epileptic boy with twisted limbs, rolling eyes, and slobbering lips, surrounded by the little group—the parents pleading, the apostles helpless, the scribes mocking. To many people that picture symbolizes their image of the Church—Christ far away on a mountaintop, attracting a few pious souls who have escaped from the valleys of life and holding them in a holy huddle while all around them is a world diseased, distracted, and desperately in need of healing. That is the image we must correct if we want the Church to become credible again to the increasing numbers of people who stand outside its life.

Meet two evangelists. One is not an evangelist any more; he dropped out of the Church's ministry in the late 1950s much to everyone's sorrow, especially mine because I admired him very much. His name is Charles Templeton and he is now a successful broadcaster and news commentator in Toronto. Charles misses no opportunity to knock the Church, partly because he wants to justify his own decision to leave it but mainly because he thinks the institutional Church has ceased to be a credible expression of Christianity. In a phone conversation that lasted nearly two hours he said to me, "There was a moment a few years ago when I thought that the Church might regain its credibility, and that was the time when ministers and priests joined the freedom marches, but it didn't last, and I didn't expect that it would. The Church serves itself, it doesn't serve the world."

The other evangelist has the same concern but he has

remained in the Church and tried to do something about it. His name is Alan Walker, and he is the Superintendent of the Central Methodist Mission in Sydney, Australia, a church that operates no less than fourteen service organizations in the community. The most exciting one is "Lifeline" which consists of some five hundred ordinary church folk who meet one evening a week to study social, moral, and emotional problems in the light of the Christian faith and who spend the rest of their discretionary time helping people who need them. Any person with any kind of problem can telephone Lifeline at any hour of the day or night, and within minutes someone will be at his side to give him friendship, counsel, or practical help and to stay with him as long as he needs. The Sydney Telephone Directory lists Lifeline among the other emergency numbers on its front page. Alan Walker believes that it is the only form of the Church that will make any front page in the future, the only form of the Church that *has* a future.

2. *A servant is someone who ministers to somebody else's needs.* "Too late!" declare the pessimists. "People don't take their needs to the Church any more; they take them to secular agencies. Once upon a time they expected and hoped to be served by the Church, but the Church did not serve them; so now the Church has lost its chance."

Howard Williams, a Baptist minister in London, makes that point in a book called *Down to Earth* [1] which shows the decline of the Church's influence in the coal-mining valleys of his native Wales. He reminds us that for many years the nonconformist chapel was the major social force in the lives of the people, but today its influence has been displaced by the influence of the Workmen's Hall. The fault of the chapel, says Dr. Williams, is that it remained

1. S.C.M. Press Ltd., London, 1964.

[53

too other-worldly and failed to touch human lives at the points where they were most grievously afflicted in *this* world. The chapel preached against poverty, injustice, and exploitation, but it did not fight those evils; it simply taught people to live with them. Really concerned Christians left the chapel and found more fruitful outlets for their social concern in the world of practical politics and labor unions.

All power to them! The more Christians in politics and labor unions, the better! But they don't put the Church out of a job. If schools, universities, hospitals, labor unions, political parties, and social agencies, within the growing framework of a welfare state, are taking over some of the Church's functions, we should rejoice that secular society is becoming more Christian in meeting the material needs of its members. It is a sign that in some measure the gospel has succeeded. Far from putting the Church out of a job, it sets the Church free to move into other areas of human need.

There are many such areas. The *Christian Century* declared editorially: "Anyone who says that the Great Society, even if it is wholly successful, will leave nothing for the churches and individual Christians to do is woefully ignorant of the immensity of the human jungle." The editorial went on to ask, "Who will free needful but foolish borrowers from the clutches of loan sharks, provide meaning for the increasingly lonely portion of our elderly society, bridge the huge voids of misunderstanding between blacks and whites in the inner cities, rescue the unemployed human wreckage floating the streets, encourage and instruct the nation's several million alcoholics, break up the stubborn formations which preserve segregated neighborhoods?"

We could expand the list and ask, Who helps secular

man to control his own lusts, and who restores his moral integrity after he has failed? Who gives him the grace to forgive and be reconciled when others have hurt him and broken his relationships? Who stirs the springs of charity in his heart and moves him to deeds of generosity and lovingkindness? Who gives him the courage to suffer? Who teaches him how to die? Man in secular society has needs that no government, labor union, or social agency can ever meet, and it is the Church's business to serve secular man at that point and minister to his needs.

3. *A servant is someone who works at somebody else's convenience.* A pastor comes to terms with that truth if he wants to be an effective pastor. Let him not try to achieve parity with other so-called "service professions," many of which don't deserve the name because they don't really serve. If you think they do, try phoning a medical specialist or the service department of a garage or the Children's Aid Society on a holiday weekend. It is possible to be professionally trained and earn a living by repairing broken bodies, broken cars, and broken homes and still not be related to the servant whom Jesus described in his parable. It is not possible to be a faithful minister of the gospel, to be professionally trained and earn a living by repairing broken souls, without being related to the servant whom Jesus described in the parable. A pastor serves people precisely at their convenience. He works while they rest and waits on tables while they eat, or else he comes into conflict with them and into conflict with himself.

I once had a capable colleague who came to the ministry from psychiatric social work and who unfortunately brought her old work-pattern with her. She sent word to one distraught person that it would be three weeks before she could give him an appointment. I suggested that by then he might have committed suicide and that she

[55

ought to see him right away. I also tried to help her see that a minister is really expected to be a servant; he helps people at their convenience, not his. Eventually she had a nervous breakdown and returned to psychiatric social work. It would have been better for her in the first place if she had followed the example of another seminary graduate who got cold feet on the eve of his ordination and opted out of the ministry because, as he said, "I want a life of my own. I don't want to be at everybody's beck and call."

What that implies for the local church was pointed out by a man who wrote an article describing a visit to a small city. Across from his hotel were two neighboring churches, impressive for their dignity and beauty but different in their external architecture. There was a more important difference. One church remained locked day and night. The writer tried several doors but never managed to get inside, though he did see its internal beauty by peeping through the windows. It seemed to be saying, "We are here to serve you but not just now. You must come to us at our convenience." The other church had its doors wide open all day and early evening. People of many ages and many types came and went continuously. It gave the impression of an ebb and flow between the street and the sanctuary. It seemed to be saying, "Come as you are and come whenever you want. We are here to serve you at your convenience." The contrast is simplistic but valid. Those two churches typify two totally different postures; and the difference between them may just decide the Church's credibility to the world outside its life.

4. *A servant is someone who does not expect to be thanked.* No need to underline what that means for the Church. In a world where nations have learned to give economic assistance to other nations who not only fail

to say "Thank you" but believe that they are conferring a favor by accepting the assistance, surely the Church can learn to serve without expecting to be thanked for it. People didn't thank Jesus because he went about doing good. A few were grateful to him, but society as a whole put him on a cross. The world often gives that treatment to those who serve it. "He was in the form of God," writes Paul, yet he "did not count equality with God a thing to be grasped, but emptied himself, taking the form of a servant, being born in the likeness of men. And being found in human form he humbled himself and became obedient unto death, even death on a cross" (Phil. 2:6–8).

I felt better able to understand Christ's self-emptying after meeting and talking with Cardinal Leger who gave up the primacy of the Roman Catholic Diocese of Montreal and went to Africa to serve in a leper colony. It was no grandstand play on his part. Quite the contrary. He did it because he wanted to share more consciously in the servant ministry of Christ. If that doesn't make sense to some people, they need to hear him say, as I did, "Only he who loves understands me." The problem for an archbishop or any top brass of the Church is that he may get his role reversed and end up being served by people instead of serving them. Paul-Emile Leger wanted to get his role straight again and he did it with remarkable success in a re-markably short time. He has divested himself of the glory of ecclesiastical office and meets you not as a prince of the Church but as a humble missionary priest. It is a Christly thing to do and it carries tremendous moral power.

What does God think of the Church as personified by Cardinal Leger? What did God think of Jesus? Paul gives the answer: "Therefore God has highly exalted him and bestowed on him the name which is above every name, that at the name of Jesus every knee should bow, in heaven

[57

"With all that Jesus came to do
and with so little time in which to do it,
why did he concentrate such a large proportion of his ministry
on comparatively few people? Poor planning!
It wouldn't have been our way at all.
We should have provided Jesus with an expert in public relations
so that he might have the maximum exposure
and his message be given the widest coverage."

ENABLING THE FEW

Chapter 4

We have this ministry . . .

Enabling the Few

No Mass Communication

"EVERY time I look at you I don't understand," cries the voice of Judas Iscariot above the crucifixion mob in the rock opera, *Jesus Christ Superstar*. What the late Judas doesn't understand is Jesus' mismanagement of his brief ministry. It was badly planned, badly timed and badly placed. If Jesus had waited a couple of millenniums and chosen a more civilized locale he could have reached a whole nation. "Israel in 4 B.C. had no mass communication." [1]

1. Copyright 1970 by Leeds Music Ltd., London, England. Sole Selling Agent Leeds Music Corporation, 445 Park Avenue, New York, N.Y.

We don't understand either. With all that Jesus came to do and with so little time in which to do it, why did he concentrate such a large proportion of his ministry on comparatively few people? Poor planning! It wouldn't have been our way at all. We should have provided Jesus with an expert in public relations, so that he might have the maximum exposure and his message be given the widest coverage. Actually a P.R. man came to Jesus and offered his services in the wilderness of temptation. Jesus said "No!" because he had not come to appeal to the many. His method was precisely to concentrate on the few.

It was one thing to make that decision in a solitary place with no people around. It must have been something else when he began his public ministry and found himself such a smashing hit with the crowds. People flocked to him by the thousands; they followed him everywhere. His friends couldn't control the demonstrations of those who came to hear him preach and to feel the touch of his healing power. Talk about "charisma"! They would have crowned him king if he had given the word, but he didn't give the word because he was not fooled by popularity. He knew how capricious crowds could be—eating out of your hand one moment and ready to eat you the next. Didn't the crowd that applauded him in the synagogue at Nazareth try to throw him headlong over a cliff when he offended their prejudices (Luke 4:29)? Wouldn't a crowd one day pollute the air with the murderous chant, "Let him be crucified" (Matt. 27:22)?

If Jesus had used our methods, if he had operated on a big scale and started a popular movement, he would have defeated his whole purpose. He came to inaugurate the Kingdom of God, God's righteous rule in human hearts and society; and, as he made crystal clear in his teachings, the Kingdom begins on a small scale, sometimes with the fraction of an attitude. So what did he do after getting rid of the P.R. man in the wilderness? The Gospel writer tells us that he walked by the Sea of Galilee and called four fishermen to follow him (Matt. 4:18–22). You can't start smaller than that, but it's where and how Christianity started—with the calling of four men from their fishing boats by the Sea of Galilee.

Later Jesus enlarged the group to twelve. He prayed all night before making that choice (Luke 6:12–16), because it was one of the most vital choices in the history of the world. He evidently had a number of followers of whom he chose twelve "to be with him." His method was not mass communication but the choice and training of a small group of men to be the link between himself and his ongoing Kingdom. And what an assortment they were! The Church has since canonized them, but they scarcely seem like suitable candidates for sainthood. Unstable Peter, hot-headed James and John, doubting Thomas, traitorous Judas, and the rest—to such ordinary men Jesus devoted the major part of his ministry and entrusted the issues of his Kingdom.

It says something for those ordinary men that they answered the call of Jesus who, after all, offered them nothing very attractive—no pay, no prestige, no political power, no promise of victory in a proletarian revolution. He simply told them that they would have to love their enemies and turn the other cheek and suffer persecution and go out as sheep in the midst of wolves. No wonder a few potential followers like the three men on the road to Jerusalem, when they realized what Jesus required of them, said, in effect, "It's not for us" (Luke 9:57–62). No wonder the rich young ruler, forced to choose between his wealth and Jesus, "went away sorrowful" (Mark 10:17–22). No wonder many of his larger circle of followers,

[63

when they came to the moment of truth, "drew back and no longer went about with him" (John 6:66). That's when the twelve proved the wisdom of Jesus in choosing them. "Will you also go away?" he asked them. "Simon Peter answered him, 'Lord, to whom shall we go? You have the words of eternal life' " (John 6:67, 68).

THE KINGDOM METHOD

The gospel ministry of Jesus actually proceeded in three stages: (1) the synagogue ministry which was terminated by the hostility of the religious leaders; (2) the open-air ministry which was, in fact, a limited exercise in mass communication; (3) the private ministry to his disciples, made necessary because a cross loomed large on the horizon, and Jesus knew that his time was running out. The watershed came on the road to Caesarea Philippi where he asked his disciples, "Who do men say that I am?" They gave him the stock answers—"John the Baptist . . . Elijah . . . one of the prophets." Then he asked, "But who do you say that I am?" Speaking for all of them, Peter blurted out, "You are the Christ" (Mark 8:27–30). From that moment Jesus focused all his powers on the training of the twelve who alone recognized that he had come from God to do the work of God and to establish God's Kingdom on earth.

To those men he addressed the main body of his teaching; and that's something to remember when we talk glibly about the "simple teachings" of Jesus, as though they were, in fact, simple to a point where any decent and civilized person can practice them. Jesus did not address his gut-level teachings to people who were just decent and civilized. He addressed them to his little group of private pupils whom he was training for the most difficult task that God ever assigned to mortal men. Take the Beatitudes with their stringent requirements of meekness, mercy, purity, and righteousness (Matt. 5:5–8). Take his tough demand for the excision of one's own hand or foot or eye if they impede entrance to the Kingdom of God (Mark 9:43–50). Take his dire warning that he came to cast fire on the earth and to cause division rather than peace (Luke 12:49–51). Take the prediction of his own passion which he followed by saying that whoever would come after him must deny himself and take up his cross and follow him (Mark 8:34). Nothing "simple" about those teachings, nothing popular. They are not broad ethical principles that can be separated from their Gospel setting. They belong to the intensive training of the small group of hand-picked men whom Jesus chose to share his ministry and carry it on after his death.

At one point Jesus put them through a kind of dress rehearsal. He sent them out on a trial run. According to Mark it happened right after his rejection at Nazareth, right after he realized the fickleness of the crowds. Calling the twelve together, he gave them instructions about their equipment, their conduct, and their demeanor and sent them out two by two with authority to teach as he taught and to heal as he healed (Mark 6:7–13). Apparently he was so encouraged by the result that soon afterwards he sent out a larger task force that numbered seventy. Subject to the same discipline as the twelve, they were to be his hands and feet and voice, going where he could not go, extending his ministry to the surrounding towns and villages.

That was his method and it proved to be fundamentally sound. It was, in fact, so stunningly successful that Jesus himself, in his own estimate of it, made one of the most hopeful statements in the Gospels. When "the seventy re-

turned with joy, saying, 'Lord, even the demons are subject to us in your name!' " he replied with greater joy, " 'I
saw Satan fall like lightning from heaven!' " (Luke 10:17–
18). In other words, here was a method that would
eventually win, a strategy that the forces of evil could
not withstand, a form of the Church against which the
gates of hell could never prevail.

It is of immense importance that we continually soak
our minds in the gospel ministry of Jesus. "We have this
ministry," wrote Paul—not some lesser ministry which
the academic gurus or the ecclesiastical bureaucrats or
the social activists or the communications experts would
foist upon the Church as a panacea to persuade the many
who stand outside its life. The Church, if it remains faithful to the ministry of Jesus, will realize that its main
business is not to persuade the many but to enable the few.
That is the Kingdom method and its pattern is plainly
outlined at the beginning of chapter nine in Luke's Gospel
which describes the first apostolic mission: "And he called
the twelve together and gave them power and authority
over all demons and to cure diseases, and he sent them out
to preach the kingdom of God and to heal" (Luke 9:1–2).

A Movement Inward

The enabling ministry of Jesus has three movements:
first, a movement inward. Jesus constituted the Church
by calling the twelve disciples out of society into a fellowship with himself at the center. That has obvious
meaning for the Church, if it seriously intends to share
and continue the gospel ministry of Jesus. First, there has
to be a calling in, a Christ-centered fellowship where Christ
is present through worship and prayer and sacrament and
pulpit proclamation. Paul employed that method in his

missionary journeys. As he traveled through the Mediter-ranean world sowing the seeds of the gospel and changing the course of history, he established little congregations in all the major cities and subsequently addressed his letters to them. The basic unit of Christianity has always been the gathered congregation of worshiping believers, and the situation has not changed even in urban society today.

We ought to ponder that truth when we hear voices deprecating the parish church. Today there seems to be almost a conspiracy against the local congregation, and it includes bishops and professors and executives and other church leaders who really ought to know better. They write books, they preach sermons, they publish pamphlets, they make radio speeches telling us that the local church has become irrelevant; it is a social anachronism, a dying organism which in its present form actually hinders the cause of Christ in the world and ought to be put to death and decently buried and forgotten. Of course, those cleri-cal morticians are still happy and anxious to feed off the corpse that they want to embalm. We might quote some of them, except that their pronouncements are so utterly mischievous and mistaken.

That is why it is refreshing to listen to the voice of Elton Trueblood who has never been a strong supporter of ecclesiastical structures, judging from his earlier books. In his more recent books the Quaker philosopher and great exponent of lay religion does a startling about-face. He gives his judgment that the time has come for the Church to put a new emphasis on its own institutional structures. He does not believe that there can ever be such a thing as "Churchless Christianity." He deplores the false dichot-omy between the idea of being a Christian in the Church and the idea of being a Christian in the world. To be sure, Christ sends us out into the world but only after he has

[67

first drawn us into the Church, because what's the use of being sent out if we have nothing to give when we arrive? There can be no available power unless it emanates from a center, and that center is the gathered fellowship where Christ is present. Trueblood writes,

> Christ's building of the little fellowship, on which depended the success of his entire enterprise, in both its endurance and its consequent penetration of the world, was the beginning of what we mean by the Church. If the faith is now forced to go on without it, the alteration in character will be so radical that what will remain will be a different reality altogether. What it may be, we naturally cannot know, but we can at least know that it will no longer be the Cause of Christ.[2]

A LATERAL MOVEMENT

Next in the enabling ministry of Jesus comes a lateral movement. Having called the twelve into a fellowship with himself at the center, Jesus "gave them power and authority over all demons and to cure diseases." That's what made Jesus different from other religious teachers. They all had their disciples who followed them and sat at their feet and listened to what they had to say, but strictly speaking Jesus did not call "disciples." He called "apostles" in order to train them for a specific task out in the world. He was no philosopher instructing his pupils on street corners. He was more like a hospital superintendent briefing his staff or even like a guerilla leader preparing and conditioning his soldiers to spearhead a revolution.

That throws new light on the role of a local church. The sociologists, to whom we paid $100,000 in Metro

2. Elton Trueblood, *The Future of the Christian* (New York and London: Harper & Row, Publishers, 1971), p. 22.

Toronto, told us that many people have turned their backs on the Church today because they see it as a purely selfish organization. They see it catering to egocentric man, man the receiver; whereas the Church ought to be an instrument for altruistic man, man the giver. So people are disillusioned, turned off, disinterested; they seek fulfillment through other service organizations. One detects the sin of pride in that criticism, a refusal to recognize that man's proper posture toward God is precisely that of a receiver. One sees also a totally wrong conception of the Church which in the New Testament sense is a fellowship where men do receive from Christ for the express purpose of having something to give to their fellowmen.

That was the conviction of Group Captain Leonard Cheshire, V.C., who after the Second World War established throughout England a chain of nursing homes for the care of the incurably ill and victims of concentration camps. Cheshire was the daredevil air ace who led the experiments in low-range bombing and accompanied the mission that dropped the first atom bomb on Hiroshima. Those experiences left a deep scar on his soul. After a tortuous spiritual pilgrimage he became a Christian and, as a first step, he joined the Church. He explains the logic of his decision: "When I became a pilot I had to learn the laws of aerodynamics and went to a training school with the authority to teach me. There I expected and found teachers to give me the facts—not their own personal ideas." Cheshire says that he expected the same thing of the Church. He was drawn to it not for selfish reasons but because he wanted to serve his fellowmen in the name of Christ and he needed to be instructed in the truths and trained in the disciplines of the Christian Faith.[3]

3. As told by Andrew Boyle in *No Passing Glory* (London: Collins, Fontana Books, 1959), p. 328.

Besides giving its members a basic training in the Bible and Christian theology, the Church might give them more specific training in the practical application of their faith. Suppose some of them came together in occupational groups to explore in the light of the New Testament what it means to continue Christ's ministry in their particular fields of work. I knew a psychiatrist who used to tell me that if he had the time he would write a book on the healing ministry of Jesus in the Gospels and make it required reading for all members of the medical profession. He saw the Man of Galilee as the greatest physician who ever practiced. He believed that doctors have much to learn from Jesus about concern for the individual, about compassion for human suffering, about accurate diagnosis, about treatment of the whole personality, about cooperation with other agencies of healing, about the physician's own sense of vocation as a servant of God. That's what we mean by the lateral movement in the Church's ministry.

The lateral movement throws new light on the role of the ordained minister who today is suffering an identity crisis. He may feel that he is up in the grandstand explaining the game to the ladies when he would really like to be with the men down on the playing field "where the action is." Before he turns in his clerical collar, however, he ought to be told that it could be the way of Christian obedience to remain for a while where the action is not. There wasn't much action for Paul in a Roman prison cell, but that's where he wrote to the apostles, prophets, evangelists, pastors, and teachers telling them of their vocation "to equip God's people for work in his service, to the building up of the body of Christ" (Eph. 4:11, 12, NEB). In Paul's view the apostles, prophets, evangelists, pastors, and teachers are not themselves the Church; they are the servants, the equippers, the enablers of the Church. There may be times for the ordained servant of God to involve himself directly in the great issues of society. There may also be times when obedience to Christ demands that he instruct, inspire, and enable his laymen who are strategically placed to do something about the great issues of society. In that view there is no grandstand; the whole Church becomes a training ground.

A Movement Outward

Third in the enabling ministry of Jesus comes a movement outward. Having called his disciples and having authorized them for their work in the world, Jesus "sent them out to preach the kingdom of God and to heal." He called them in and trained them for the express purpose of sending them out again. He established the Church not for its own sake, not to save its own life, not simply to survive, but to lose itself in loving service to all humanity.

That has many implications for the Church today, not least of all that a church which consciously continues Christ's ministry will accept more than one standard of success. Most of us who are middle-aged have grown up with a fairly fixed image of a successful church. We picture a building bulging with enthusiastic members who schedule their multiple Sunday morning services like a railway timetable. We picture a building which is a beehive of bustling activity all week long, lights burning every night in all the rooms, programs for every age and interest group. Not long ago I preached in such a church which consists of a complex of buildings, like a college campus, that were constructed within the past few years at a cost of three and a half million dollars on nineteen and a half acres of land. Its membership exceeds twenty-four hundred and is growing, and its annual budget exceeds four hundred thousand dollars. By at least one standard we could call it a

[71

successful church, and we hope that in our urban society there will always be churches that measure up to that standard.

But surely that doesn't have to be our only image of a successful church. Here is another congregation, not large numerically but composed of people who know and care for one another as persons and take their fellowship in Christ seriously. They come together on Sundays, perhaps in a sacred building, perhaps in a building used for many different purposes. They worship but they make no fuss over it. They regard worship not as an end in itself but as a means of enabling them to perform a Christian ministry out in the world. They worship to commune with Christ and hear his Word, so that he may instruct and inspire them to be his hands, his feet, his voice, the instruments of his continuing ministry. One of their number, who may or may not be ordained but who is gifted and qualified as a teacher, counselor, and stirrer-up of hearts, briefs and encourages his fellow-Christians in their ministry. They sing hymns and listen to music that binds them to God and deepens their desire to be used by him. They meet together in small groups to share their insights and to pray. When the worship ends, the service begins. Having called them into his Church and having enabled them to serve him, Christ sends his disciples out into the world's life to be his witnesses by word and example, to proclaim his gospel and to continue his ministry among men.

Both those churches play a vital role in the work of God's Kingdom, and we cannot say that one is more relevant than the other. Social patterns change, however, and churches change if they don't want to become museums. The big, busy, bulging building belonged to an era when people had less money to spend and less leisure time, and families stayed home together on weekends, and mothers didn't go out to work, and there were fewer adult toys, and the Church was a big deal in people's lives. Perhaps now we have entered the era of smaller churches, though not necessarily of weaker churches. After all, if the Church shares faithfully in the gospel ministry of Jesus, if it makes the demands that he made and does not dispense what Bonhoeffer called "cheap grace," it can never expect to be more than a creative minority. I say a *creative* minority, because although small, the Church can be strong out of all proportion to its size like salt in food, yeast in bread, a beam of light in the darkness—Christ's own figures of speech. The Church was never stronger than when it consisted of thirteen men in a fishing boat on the Sea of Galilee.

At the funeral of Sir Winston Churchill, the procession was headed by a single rank of middle-aged men wearing the faded uniforms of the Royal Air Force. They were all that remained of the few hundred young Englishmen flying small fighter aircraft who beat back the Luftwaffe in 1940 and held the pass for Western civilization. Churchill himself paid them the most deathless tribute by saying, "Never . . . was so much owed by so many to so few." When the saints march into heaven, the procession will be headed by some of the men in that small fishing boat. Close to them will be the faithful company who stood firm against the secular culture and held the pass for the Christian Church in the 1970s; and later generations at the rear of the procession may be heard to say gratefully, "Never was so much owed by so many to so few."

*"In obedience to the great commission of its Lord,
the Church, if it hopes to remain afloat,
must always head out to the open sea of God's world."*

REACHING OUT

Chapter 5

We have this ministry . . .

Reaching Out

I HAVE a friend in Toronto who has distinguished him-self as a ham radio operator. Let me confess that I always thought of amateur broadcasting as the rather selfish and extravagant hobby of an electronic elite. I thought of the ham as an antisocial character, holed up in his "shack," surrounded by a jungle of expensive equipment and mut-tering messages into a microphone that no ordinary person could understand. An afternoon spent at my friend's house, listening and talking over his station, made nonsense of all those ideas.

To be sure, the ham operates alone in a confined space, but his lines of communication extend all over the world. He belongs to a unique fellowship whose four hundred thousand members include all kinds of people from bank presidents to service station attendants. They talk with one another on the air waves, they exchange news and stories, always on a high level, and sometimes they do serious things like Bible study at six o'clock in the morning. They are an enabling fellowship whose members help one another get started and who are particularly anxious to initiate their children, because it has been proved that when young people become absorbed in ham radio they have no time for drugs, demonstrations, and eccentric life styles.

Hams give vital service to the community such as providing emergency communication in hurricanes, blackouts, and blizzards. Since 1967 a small group of them have given thousands of hours of spare time and provided costly materials at their own expense to assemble and install stations for the blind. Thanks to them there are now 150 blind hams in Canada. One of them, with whom I chatted over the microphone, told me that, after living in lonely darkness for twenty years, he now sees by means of ham radio farther than he could see when he had physical sight. He said it was like being raised from the dead. In my friend's house that afternoon I discovered to my great surprise that what I had thought to be a tight little circle is, in fact, one of the most unselfish and outgoing fraternities in the world.

I wish that more people could make the same discovery about the Church. Too many think of Christianity as the selfish and extravagant hobby of a religious elite. They think of Church people as being rather antisocial, holed up in their sanctuaries, surrounded by expensive organs and stained glass windows, and muttering messages to one another in a jargon that no ordinary person understands. They need to spend some time in the Church and learn that its lines of communication extend across the world. They need to learn that Christians have a large and unique fellowship that includes people more widely separated than bank presidents and service station attendants. They need to learn that it is an enabling fellowship whose members help one another to get started and who are particularly anxious to initiate their children, because it has been proved that when young people become absorbed in Jesus Christ they have no time for drugs, demonstrations, and eccentric life styles. They need to discover that the Church has always been ready with emergency help in times of disaster and that Christian people have a special concern for the blind, the defective, and all the handicapped members of our society. A lot of folk, if they spent an afternoon at the Church, might discover to their great surprise that what they thought to be a tight little circle is, in fact, the most unselfish and outgoing fraternity in the world.

How can it be otherwise if the Church consciously continues the ministry of Jesus in the Gospels? He had his little fraternity, the few disciples whom he chose and trained, but he did not restrict his ministry to the few. He continually reached out not only beyond the boundaries of his own circle but beyond the boundaries of race, religion, and social class. He had a particular personal concern for those whom he called "the lost sheep of the house of Israel." That's what made him so unpopular with the orthodox rabbis. Jewish society in the first century designated certain groups of people as "outsiders" and expected them to be treated as such, especially by religious teachers. There were foreigners like the Canaanite woman whose daughter Jesus healed (Matt. 15:21–28), and the Roman centurion whose faith he commended (Luke 7:1–10). There were tax collectors like Matthew whom he called as a disciple (Mark 2:14), and sinners like the woman taken in adultery whom he saved from the murderous mob (John 8:1–11). There were the women who followed

[79

him to the cross (Luke 23:27), and the little children to whom he gave his blessing (Mark 10:13–16). Such "outsiders" were his special concern. He compared himself to a shepherd with a hundred sheep in his flock who is willing to leave ninety-nine in the fold while he goes out into the wilderness to seek and to save one lost animal. He said, "For the Son of man came to seek and to save the lost" (Luke 19:10).

Jesus committed that outreach ministry to his Church. In fact, the last thing that the Risen Christ said to his disciples, before leaving their earthly presence, was, "You shall be my witnesses in Jerusalem and in all Judea and Samaria and to the end of the earth" (Acts 1:8). Having said that, he vanished from their sight. They were on their own now. Henceforth they would have to carry on his ministry sustained only by his spiritual presence. Nor could there be any doubt as to the thrust of that ministry. It must not be introverted and confined to the nurture of the in-group but must reach out with compassionate concern for all who stand outside the community of faith. It must begin at home, reach throughout the country, extend even to their enemies, and finally stretch across the whole earth.

In one of George Bernard Shaw's plays a sea captain cries out, "The Church is on the rocks. I told them that it would be unless it headed for God's open sea." In obedience to the great commission of its Lord, the Church, if it hopes to remain afloat, must always head out to the open sea of God's world. Consider what that means for the Church today by looking closely at three honored words —outreach, evangelism, and mission.

Outreach

No need to argue the importance of outreach. The very

word crops up with almost monotonous frequency in the conversation of concerned Christians. All intelligent people know that the Church cannot survive as a closed spiritual society in a wide open secular world. You still find a few private religious clubs that try to operate on a "Members Only" policy, but they are dying. A friend of mine dropped into one of them for Sunday worship. He had a wide choice of empty pews but, being a friendly fellow, he chose a pew with one other occupant, a well-dressed lady. He smiled at her and started to put his hat on the vacant place beside him, but she leaned over and whispered, "That is my husband's seat." My friend apologized and quickly removed his hat and laid it on the floor. The space beside him remained vacant, so he could not help remarking after the service, "Your husband didn't come." The woman replied frostily, "My husband is dead." My friend decided that it was a new angle on the communion of saints and may have partially explained why that particular church seemed more dead than alive.

Yet whoever assumes that such comic situations are normal today, whoever clings to the image of the Church as a holy huddle of pious people with no concern for anyone but themselves, simply betrays the fact that he has not been in firsthand contact with the Church for a long time. We marvel at such half-truths as that voiced by the executive director of the Canadian Welfare Council who said that "some of the most stubborn opponents of anti-poverty measures and the toughest critics of the poor . . . are to be found among the faithful in their pews on Sunday." [1] It is also true that some of the most stubborn supporters of antipoverty measures and some of the staunchest friends of the poor are to be found among the faithful in their

1. Reported in the *Globe and Mail*, Toronto, Feb. 19, 1969.

[81

pews on Sunday. The whole truth is that their posture toward poverty is decided precisely by their presence in the pews.

Of all the moneys which Canadian people and organizations contributed to the Nigeria-Biafra Relief Fund in 1968 more than half were raised in and by the churches. Yet in the light of that fact a secular newspaper in my city published a "Manifesto on Poverty" which recommended among other things the immediate closure and sale of many church buildings.[2] It was the Judas-mentality: "Why all this waste?" The proceeds might underwrite our welfare budget for a few weeks; *then* where do we turn? Jesus said, "You always have the poor with you, and whenever you will, you can do good to them, but you will not always have me" (Mark 14:7). Disregarding the fact that churches, unlike many other institutions, make no demands on the public purse, how can they be expected to reach out and help the poor if they have no centers of motive and faith and inspiration to reach out from?

For several years I have received a letter each Christmas from a Church of South India pastor who rejoices in the musical name of Sam Devapragasam. Sam is what I consider to be a balanced Christian. He believes in prayer and he believes in outreach. After his retirement he and his wife, Nesam, went to a remote part of the country where, with no resources but their faith in God's providence, they built and opened a hostel for the housing and education of orphaned and unwanted children. God has provided for them and blessed their work beyond all expectation. Gifts have poured in from interested friends all over the world, and the investment has paid rich dividends in terms of

2. *Toronto Star*, June 28, 1969.

young lives redeemed from hopelessness and trained for useful careers.

In a recent letter Nesam writes, "I am happy to report that as many as seventy orphan children have been educated by us and employed as teachers, mechanics, midwives, carpenters, etc. . . . Thirty-four of our children have been married . . . their family life is one of happiness and peace." In the same letter Sam asks why he and his wife should be doing such work at a time when they have earned the right to take life easy. He says, "A simple answer is, 'Because God cares and loves.' " He adds, "The time has come when the Church needs to identify itself with the problems facing it, viz., poverty, hunger, under-development, etc. The Church should be the Church of the poor and the needy and not just of a privileged section of mankind."

That very recognition, which derives not from sociology but from the New Testament, has opened an exciting new chapter in the Church's life all over the world. No knowledgeable and sympathetic observer of the local congregation can fail to notice the radical change of emphasis over the past ten years, the departure from traditional programs and the new concern for outreach, not as an alternative to the worship and nurture that preserve the Church's historic identity but as the logical outgrowth of Christian worship and nurture. Today many churches operate nurseries for retarded children, programs for elderly folk, language schools for immigrants, summer day-camps for boys and girls, drop-in centers for drop-out youth—all with the earnest intention to reach out and serve people in the community, most of whom will never attend a service of worship or put a dollar in the collection plate. Those who write about the new projects or dramatize them on tele-

vision like to play up the opposition of the few reaction-
aries who reluctantly pay the bills and resent the dirty
footprints on their clean church floors. They neglect to
mention that the majority of Christian folk support and
help the outreach programs and do so with a sense of being
privileged to share in the gospel ministry of Jesus.

EVANGELISM

But the word *outreach* has its limitations. To many
church folk it means nothing more than making their
buildings freely available to outside organizations or siphon-
ing off funds to finance work for other people to do in the
community. It suggests a form of practical service which
may be the duty of concerned Christians but is not ex-
clusively Christian. Jesus served people in a practical way
but he didn't always begin there and he never stopped
there. Beyond filling their empty stomachs with bread he
filled their empty lives with meaning. Beyond healing their
wounded bodies he healed their wounded spirits. Beyond
giving them the Golden Rule he forgave them for breaking
the Golden Rule. Beyond helping them to be more human
he helped them to be more like God. That ministry also
he committed to his Church, and we can call it by no other
name than "evangelism."

Unfortunately the word *evangelism* has fallen on bad
days. Some churches seem hysterically anxious to purge it
from their vocabularies, not only because it belongs to the
language of "Christianese" which no one outside the
Church apparently understands, but because the whole
idea of evangelism has become slightly unrespectable. It
suggests proselytizing of the more vulgar variety; and in a
pluralist society that prides itself on its tolerance the
"Have-you-been-saved-my-brother?" approach becomes

offensive. We now consider it our Christian duty not to convert the outsider but to coexist with him and dialogue with him and persuade him that we consider his point of view as valid as ours. Oddly enough, the rival secular faiths have no such reticence. They coexist, they dialogue, but only as a means of breaking down our defenses and winning us over to their point of view. The Communists and humanists frankly evangelize, they "compass land and sea to make one proselyte," they infiltrate our whole culture with their materialistic philosophies which aim to create a world without God. In that situation it is strange indeed that the Church should cease to evangelize—unless, of course, the Church has lost its nerve, or its gospel.

Perhaps we have really lost our imagination. We are so conditioned by the old techniques that we still see evangelism as the hard-sell pressure on outsiders to become insiders. That was certainly the motive behind the "visitation evangelism" campaigns in the 1950s when legions of laymen, armed with promotion pamphlets, blitzed their neighborhoods and invited people to come to church. The people responded, and the campaigns succeeded, as far as they went, but where have all those people gone? Perhaps next time we ought to offer our products in different order. Instead of selling the Church in the hope that, once inside it people will buy the gospel, we might try to sell the gospel in the hope that, once it takes possession of people they will feel drawn to the Church. *That* is evangelism.

When I returned from England after spending six years as a minister in London, I brought back a gloomy picture of the state of the Christian religion in that country. On reflection I realize that, though church life is distressingly weak in Britain, the gospel is still being communicated to the world outside the Church, sometimes more effectively than on this side of the Atlantic. Courses on religion, with

[85

academic credits, are offered as options to all boys and girls in private and state-supported schools. The weekend newspapers present articles on serious spiritual subjects with little or no reference to the lunatic fringe of religion. Many of the leading publishers include religious titles in their best-seller lists. The British Broadcasting Corporation and the independent networks have large, well-staffed religion departments which present daily and weekly programs on radio and television that attract millions of listeners and viewers by their maturity and imagination. People may not go to church in Britain, but the gospel is being proclaimed, and *that* is evangelism.

In 1956 the General Council of the United Church of Canada met in Windsor, Ontario, just across the river from Detroit. In its report the *Christian Century* described us as being "in many ways the most complete and vital Protestant communion in North America." Why did we deserve that extravagant tribute which may or may not be valid today? Apparently because of our passion for evangelism which at that time was very strong. The *Century*, which also at that time had a passion for evangelism, went on to say, "No church assembly south of the border provides a comparable sense of the church struggling for the soul of the nation." [3] A week later the same city of Windsor became the scene of the struggle in the first National Evangelistic Mission which lasted eight days during which thirty thousand people attended services in the hockey arena and several hundred made decisions for Christ. That was my only attempt to fill the shoes of Billy Graham, and, though I didn't fit them very well, I never had a stronger sense of sharing in the gospel ministry

3. *The Christian Century*, Oct. 3, 1956, p. 1125.

of Jesus. I came away with the burning conviction that by one technique or another the Church must continually reach out with the gospel of Jesus Christ and confront men and women at the point of decision. *That* is evangelism, and *that* is our ministry.

MISSION

The third and most honored word is *mission.* If the Church ever drops that word from its vocabulary it will have written its own obituary, and its buildings will be like war memorial museums, related to the past but not to the present and future. Outreach, evangelism, and mission are not optional activities like bowling, billiards, and Ping-Pong for the members of a religious club. They are mandates from Christ himself, a part of the original givenness of the gospel. The Church does not engage in mission; the Church *is* mission, or it ceases to be the Church.

It is no accident that the periods of great strength in the Church's life have been the periods when it consciously continued the ministry of Christ in obedience to his commission: "You shall be my witnesses in Jerusalem and in all Judea and Samaria and to the end of the earth." That was especially true of the "Great Century" of the world missionary movement which unhappily has come to a close in our lifetime. Christians and non-Christians who denigrate it as arrogant paternalism or cultural imperialism, those who equate it with the worst features of colonialism and hold it responsible for the tension in East-West relations, allow their own prejudices to blind them to the facts. The fact is that no single endeavor in Church history has been so heroic, adventurous, sacrificial, and productive. Of the 818 million people who, according to a United

[87

Nations projection, will be living in Africa in the year 2000, five hundred million may be members of the Christian Church. Someone has said that with the compelling assurance of its faith the nineteenth century drew back the arm of its strength and hurled the beneficent boomerang of missions across Asia, Africa, and the Islands of the Sea. Now the boomerang has come back bringing challenge to us in the Western world to measure up to the very gospel which we persuaded other peoples to accept.

In my mind the great name synonymous with the missionary movement of the past hundred years is Hudson Taylor, founder of the China Inland Mission. On a Sunday morning in 1865 he rushed out of a crowded church in Brighton, England, gasping for air, because the atmosphere of smug piety made him feel physically ill. His thoughts at that moment were far away in China. Describing the experience, he said, "Unable to bear the sight of a congregation of a thousand or more Christian people rejoicing in their own security, while millions were perishing for lack of knowledge, I wandered out on the sands alone in great spiritual agony."

There was another occasion, after Hudson Taylor had been to China, when he was addressing a conference of church people in Scotland. He shocked them with the story of some Chinese fishermen who allowed a man to drown because the man's wife would not pay them sufficient money to pull him out of the water. Taylor paused to let the picture sink in. Sensing the hot indignation of his audience, he continued quietly, "Is the body, then, of so much more value than the soul? We condemn those heathen fishermen. We say that they were guilty of the man's death—because they could easily have saved him, and did not do it. But what of the millions whom we leave to perish and that eternally? What of the plain command, "Go ye into all the world and preach the gospel to every creature'?"[4]

Yes, what about it—right now? Granted that a host of external factors, such as the closing of national frontiers and the resurgence of ethnic religions, discourage and even prohibit missionary outreach in the old-fashioned sense, does the Church still take seriously the commission of Christ to preach his gospel abroad and save the souls of men? Or have we changed our strategy completely and turned what used to be warm-blooded missionary outreach into juiceless social service? Have we decided that the Church really continues the *whole* of Christ's ministry simply by cooperating with secular agencies in helping underdeveloped peoples to build schools, combat disease, drill wells, and increase the crop-yield of their land? Are we satisfied to send abroad our doctors, nurses, teachers, industrialists, and engineers but not our evangelists for fear that they will be declared persona non grata by the kind of people to whom Christ proclaimed the gospel of God's love?

Some church leaders are not satisfied. When the Central Committee of the World Council of Churches convened at Lucknow in the 1950s, the members were welcomed by a high official of the Indian government who shocked them by saying brusquely and condescendingly that, while his country had benefited from the schools and appreciated the hospitals which Christian missionaries had established, never again would there be room for proselytizing. That was an offensive kind of cultural imperialism that had to stop. The late Dr. Franklin Clark Fry, who was Chairman of the Central Committee, replied graciously. He told the

4. Told by J. C. Pollock in *Hudson Taylor and Maria* (London: Hodder & Stoughton, 1962), pp. 133, 139.

[89

official that Christians had come to India as friends and that the mark of a friend is that he feels the compulsion to share his best. Clinics and colleges are good, he went on to say, and we have been glad to give them; but good as they are, the minds they train will be empty and the lives they preserve will be a mockery, if it all ends there. The best is the joy that can be bright only as it flames from peace of soul, a peace which in turn can be strong and serene only when it issues from hope, a hope which is fruit that grows only on the vine of a living faith in Jesus Christ. That is the best we have to give, and if we are true friends we must reach out and give it.

"The word whole *expresses a truth about the purpose
of Jesus' healing ministry that no other word can express. . . .
Jesus treated people as whole persons.
He never left a man well in body but unwell in spirit.
On the other hand, if he saw that a man's spiritual sickness
had its roots in a physical cause . . .
he dealt with that cause first."*

MAKING PEOPLE WELL

Chapter 6

We have this ministry . . .

Making People Well

The Great Physician

IN A TENDER and moving biography James Davidson Ross tells about the migraine headaches which his beloved wife, Clare, suffered from the time of her youth. The attacks came every two or three weeks, of such intensity that she could not lift a finger for twenty-four hours; and the pain was so excruciating that it put her vision out of focus and distorted her speech. Doctors offered no hope of cure. The only thing to be done for her was to get her to bed as quickly as possible, darken the room and leave her alone to suffer.

While Clare, in middle-age, was still feeling sick and wretched in the aftermath of one of her worst attacks, her husband took her to a Chapel of Divine Healing where she prayed and received the laying on of hands. She left the chapel with all signs of migraine gone, and to the end of her life she never had another attack. Her husband writes, "The cynic may say that a psychosomatic complaint had been dealt with by psychological means: the cynic may say what he will. . . . In faith Clare had taken twenty years of sickness to God, and in faith she had left that sickness with him." [1]

A Chapel of Divine Healing—that's what every church must become if it hopes to share the whole ministry of Jesus in the Gospels. It was a healing ministry; and we mustn't gloss over that fact or leave its recognition to Mary Baker Eddy. The Gospels, especially that written by Luke, himself a doctor, portray Jesus as the Great Physician who moved among sick people and made them well. It wasn't a matter of performing miracles but of ministering to the total needs of people. Jesus believed that God had sent and empowered him not only to save men from evil but to save them from disease and death and all the manifestations of evil's power. That's how he interpreted his role as God's Messiah. When John the Baptist, brooding in his prison cell, sent messengers of doubt with the pathetic question, "Are you he who is to come, or shall we look for another?" Jesus replied, "Go and tell John what you have seen and heard: the blind receive their sight, the lame walk, lepers are cleansed, and the deaf hear, the dead are raised up, the poor have good news preached to them" (Luke 7:18–22).

The people to whom Jesus extended his healing ministry seem to fall into three groups. The first group included

1. James Davidson Ross, *Clare* (London: Hodder and Stoughton, 1965), pp. 53–4, 130–31.

blind Bartimaeus (Mark 10:46–52), the epileptic boy
(Mark 9:14–29), the ten lepers (Luke 17:11–19), the
centurion's servant (Matt. 8:5–10), the nobleman's son
(John 4:46–53), the woman in the crowd (Mark 5:24–34)
and the daughter of Jairus (Mark 5:21–43)—all of whom
suffered from physical, organic ailments which were in-
curable by the medical practice of that time. The second
group included the paralytic whose friends lowered him
through the roof (Matt. 9:2–8), the Gadarene demoniac
(Mark 5:1–20) and perhaps the cripple by the Pool of
Bethesda (John 5:1–13)—who suffered organic symptoms
but whom Jesus treated in mind as well as body and for
whom he prescribed some kind of spiritual therapy. The
third group Jesus himself designated when he told the
Pharisees, "Those who are well have no need of a physician, but those who are sick; I came not to call the righteous, but sinners." (Mark 2:17). Those "sick" people whom
he called and made well included such sinners as the
adulterous Samaritan woman (John 4:1–42), Mary the
Bethany prostitute (Luke 7:36–50), Zacchaeus the dishon-
est tax collector (Luke 19:1–10), and the penitent thief
who died with him on Calvary (Luke 23:39–43).

There is at least one respect in which modern transla-
tions of the Bible do not improve on the sense of the
King James Version. In the King James account of the
healing by the Pool of Bethesda Jesus asked the crippled
man, "Wilt thou be made whole?" Whenever the Gospel
writers refer to actual healing they use that same word
whole. Jesus said to the woman in the crowd who
touched the hem of his garment, "Daughter, thy faith hath
made thee whole." The word *whole* expresses a truth
about the purpose of Jesus' healing ministry that no other
word can express. In our idiom, when we describe someone as "a whole person," we mean that he is a healthy

[95

person in all or most of the elements of his personality. Jesus treated people as whole persons. He never left a man well in body but unwell in spirit. On the other hand, if he saw that a man's spiritual sickness had its roots in a physical cause—hunger, pain, disease, infirmity—he dealt with that cause first. Jesus came to make people well. That was the ministry which he began during his earthly career.

Empowered to Heal

The healing ministry of Jesus did not end with his earthly career; it continued through the disciples whom he had trained and empowered. Peter and John go through the temple gate at the hour of prayer where a crippled beggar asks them for a handout. They have no money but they do for him what gold and silver cannot do: they straighten his twisted limbs and give him the strength to walk. Peter tells the marveling spectators not to marvel and says, in effect, "We didn't do this miracle. Christ did it. You thought you had killed Christ by nailing him to a cross. You put him to death, but God raised him from the dead. He is alive now and continuing his ministry through us" (Acts 3:1–16).

On the night before his crucifixion Jesus made a staggering promise to his fearful disciples in the Upper Room: "Truly, truly, I say to you, he who believes in me will also do the works that I do; and greater works than these will he do, because I go to the Father" (John 14:12). What comes as promise in the Gospels appears as fact in the Acts of the Apostles. The disciples continued their Master's healing ministry without interruption, performing not only his works but greater works than he had performed. They made the lame walk, restored sight to the blind, and even raised the dead to life. People brought their sick on beds and stretchers and left them in the street so that even the shadow of the disciples might fall upon them and heal them (Acts 5:15).

Wherever the Church has been faithful to its Lord, it has continued his ministry of making men well. It is no accident that through the centuries the work of healing has received its main impetus from the Church, no accident that some monasteries were places of healing and that many hospitals began as religious foundations. It is no accident that Christian missionaries, going abroad to proclaim the gospel, have taken with them the knowledge, the skill, the equipment, and the sympathy to heal the sick and build clinics and teach people how to combat disease. Behind it all is the recognition that, because Christ is concerned for man's total welfare, the Church in obedience to Christ must share that concern and be committed to his ministry of making men whole.

Someone, who evidently believes in the Lordship of Christ, has dared to suggest that all the skills and powers of modern medical science really represent the continued healing ministry of Christ. That thought possessed me on the one occasion when I was privileged to witness an open heart operation performed by one of the world's most brilliant surgeons. The patient was a six-year-old child, the daughter of a truckdriver. The doctor described her to me as "a serious case" but said that she might have a normal life if his surgery proved successful. From the balcony I saw her lying unconscious on the table, dwarfed by the awesome equipment of man's inventive genius and surrounded by a team of doctors and nurses who combined the concentrated medical prowess of the centuries. Swiftly they made a great gaping hole in the little child's chest, separated the rib cage and laid bare her beating heart, preparing her for the critical operation. When the surgeon

[97

himself approached the table and took her heart in his skillful hands, I felt sure that I was looking at the healing hands of Christ and I wanted to kneel down and pray. It was a profoundly religious experience.

"THE CHURCH IS HEALING"

Look now at the Church's role in relation to the three groups of people whom Jesus healed. First, the physically ill. Someone may ask, "What can the Church do for them any more?" Medicine, like other areas of man's life, has become largely secularized. The Church may have a role in physical healing, but it is peripheral and rapidly diminishing. It was spelled out to me in my first rural pastorate when I visited my first sick parishioner, a dying man in a tar-paper shack. As I arrived I met the doctor who had come thirty miles from the nearest town. He said, "Well, Reverend, there's nothing more I can do for him. It's up to you now." That's the familiar image of the role of religion in physical healing—a last-resort measure to be tried when all other resources have been exhausted. When medicine fails and drugs won't work and surgery is useless and the doctors give up hope, *then* we turn to Christian Science, faith-healing missions, prayers for the sick, and Roman Catholic miracle shrines. God fills the gaps, but the gaps are getting narrower.

There is an interesting little book that speaks to this situation, entitled *The Church Is Healing*.[2] Its author is Michael Wilson, once a medical doctor practicing in West Africa and now an ordained Church of England priest. Dr. Wilson, who believes that a Communion chalice and a kidney basin are equally sacred, does not believe that secu-

2. London: S.C.M. Press, 1966.

larism has driven God out of medicine. He believes that God is still present wherever there is healing but that we have to meet him in a new way. Instead of trying to bring God from the outside into a situation of sickness, we must look for him inside that situation, find out what he is doing and cooperate with him at that point.

Dr. Wilson cites the example of lobar pneumonia where our ancestors anxiously prayed for the coming of the crisis (usually about the sixth day) when sudden sweat and drop in temperature took the patient out of danger. Today, with penicillin, the crisis is predictable and occurs within a few hours. Says Dr. Wilson, "Instead of interceding for the cure of pneumonia, we must learn to give thanks for antibiotics; and pray that those who use them will do so responsibly toward God, and skillfully and lovingly toward men" (p. 58).

Though he insists that religion is no substitute for medicine, Dr. Wilson insists also that medicine is only one factor in the healing of the whole man. There is also a human factor which in the relation of a doctor to his patient can make all the difference between slow and quick recovery, sometimes between life and death. If the doctor himself is "a whole person" and does not have illusions of infallibility, he will not assume that he can cure everything with surgery and drugs in the same way that a garage mechanic tackles engine repair. Nor will he regard himself as the Great Healer. He will humbly recognize that he is *one* member of a healing team which includes his colleagues, the interns, the nurses, the technicians, the orderlies, the patient's family, pastor, and friends and the patient himself. Through all the members of that team, as they respect one another and work together, the Great Physician continues his ministry of healing.

Dr. Wilson does not like to see the Church's healing

[99

ministry turned into a cult with its own language, ritual, and protected areas. He insists that the healing of the whole person is the business of the whole Church, not just the specialty of a few fanatics. He compares it to the word *mission* which used to be associated with special societies, special collections, and special journeys to a far country but which in this ecumenical era is recognized as the life and breath of the whole Church. We no longer talk of missions as a specialized activity of the Church, we don't even say that the Church *has* missions, we say that the Church *is* mission or it ceases to be the Church.

In the same way, says Dr. Wilson, the word *healing* needs to be rescued from the specializers. We must not say that the Church engages in healing but that the Church itself *is* healing. The words *Church* and *healing* should be synonymous. When Dr. Wilson writes of the Church he refers particularly to the local congregation, and he quotes a formal statement made by missionary doctors from all over the world who met in Germany in 1964 under the auspices of the World Council of Churches:

If healing is understood as above, it will be clear that the entire congregation has a part to play in it. By its prayer, by the love with which it surrounds each person, by the practical acts which express its concern for every man, and by the opportunities which it offers for participation in Christ's mission, the congregation is the primary agent of healing. At the heart of this healing activity lies the ministry of Word, Sacraments and prayer. The specialized work of those who have been trained in the techniques of modern medicine have their proper place and will be fruitful in the context of this whole congregational life. . . . One of the most urgent needs of today is that Christian congregations, in collaboration with Christian medical workers, should again recognize and exercise the healing ministry which belongs properly to them (p. 82).

"THE HEALING OF PERSONS"

The Church plays a very important role in the healing of emotional illness. That is not the same as mental illness which requires highly skilled attention, although we can be instructed by the director of a mental hospital in England who says concerning the therapies that counteract nervous diseases, "I would undoubtedly give first place to the simple habit of prayer." Christ commissioned his Church to make men whole, and we have already noted that medicine alone cannot cure the ills of the whole personality. Medicine may cure a patient's illness but not heal the patient himself. In fact, a success from a surgical point of view could possibly be a failure from a human point of view. What is accomplished by giving an aging cancer patient a new lease on life if it simply returns him to being a selfish old man who spends his reprieve from hell making life a hell for everybody else?

Dr. Paul Tournier, the Swiss psychiatrist, is a devout Christian who firmly believes that some illnesses have such deep emotional roots that *only* Christ can heal them. In his book, *The Healing of Persons*, he describes a visit to a hypochondriac in a hospital. " 'My dear friend,' " he said, " 'I have come to tell you frankly what is the matter with you.' " With unremitting frankness he pinpointed the patient's problem as a psychotic sense of guilt over a tragedy for which he felt responsible.

" 'You have come to a crossroads,' " said Dr. Tournier. " 'I have no doubt that God has brought you to this present moment so that you can make your choice. There are two

[101

roads in front of you. One goes from clinic to clinic; it is full of suffering, but is relatively easy to take. It is the road along which you expect healing to come from others, from doctors clever enough to discover some new remedy which will cure you.

" 'The other road is very much harder. It is the road to Jesus Christ, who has warned us that it is a narrow and difficult one. If you take it, you must accept what comes to you, carry your cross, put up with your troubles, have the courage to go back to work, and face up to life even though it hurts. It is a road which demands a change of heart. But you do not travel it alone; and even if it demands the greatest sacrifices, you will find joy in it, because as you go you will find that Christ is at your side, and sins are forgiven.' " [3]

One of the fine features of the City Temple in London, where I served as pastor for a few years, is the psychological clinic started by my distinguished predecessor, Dr. Leslie Weatherhead, who himself is a qualified practicing psychologist. In his writings and in his ministry Dr. Weatherhead demonstrated the role that a local church can play in the healing of persons. The clinic itself is a loosely knit body of psychiatrists, physicians, psychologists, and pastors who serve on a voluntary or semivoluntary basis, seeing the patients sometimes in their offices, sometimes in the clinic rooms at the church. An emotionally disturbed person who comes to the City Temple seeking help is interviewed by one of the ministers who refers him to the medical specialist most likely to help him. It's not a buck-passing process, because the members of the clinic are committed Christians who work together

3. Paul Tournier, *The Healing of Persons* (New York: Harper & Row, Publishers, 1965), p. 217.

as a team. The medical men keep in touch with the pastor and use the pastor when it appears that his counseling skills may be valuable.

A young theological graduate, who did not believe in Gay Liberation, confided to me that his problem deterred him from being ordained. I sent him to Dr. Ernest White, who was an expert in dealing with that abnormality. After seeing him regularly for a period of six months, Dr. White sent him back to me for spiritual and vocational counsel. Today the young man is an effective and well-adjusted minister.

Many emotionally disturbed people do not need medical help at all. More than anything else in the world they need to be understood and accepted by a community of caring Christians. With or without a psychological clinic any congregation is capable of continuing the healing ministry of Christ to men and women in their fears, guilts, hates, depression, and anxiety. There came to the church which I served a young girl in her early twenties who had a right to be emotionally disturbed and a right to hate the church. When she was a child her parents' marriage broke up disastrously. She went to live with her grandfather who was a minister and not a very good minister. Even in middle-age he could not remain faithful to one wife and was eventually discharged from his profession. That home also broke up, and the poor girl, still in her early teens, had to make her own way in the world. Yet, in spite of her unattractive presence and moody temperament, the young people of the church accepted her and surrounded her with affectionate concern.

Gradually in that therapeutic environment the girl began to change. Her hard attitude softened. Her personality became more outgoing. She learned to trust and smile. In time one of the most emotionally balanced young men

[103

in the church proposed to her, and her happiness became complete in the secure love of Christian marriage. Obviously churches cannot always promise *that* miracle but they should be able to promise the conditions that make it possible.

HEALING THE UN-SICK

The Church continues Christ's ministry to the morally sick. One of the more humane insights of recent years is that alcoholics, drug addicts, sex perverts, compulsive gamblers, and many other moral offenders, whom we once designated as bad people, are, in fact, sick people and should be treated as such. They can no more control their harmful and degrading habits than a patient with chronic bronchitis can control his repulsive coughing. Some guardians of the law complain that we have gone too far in our eagerness to exonerate criminals of moral responsibility for their crimes. One of them was heard to say about a man accused of murder, "Oh yes, he'll be judged guilty until the do-gooders and the bleeding hearts start writing to the newspapers, 'Pity the poor fellow. Considering his unhappy background, how dare we expect him *not* to go about hitting old ladies with lead pipes?'" Yet with full allowance for error in the direction of leniency, it is still true that our society comes closer to the spirit of Jesus by recognizing that sinners are not always bad people who need to be punished; sometimes they are sick people who need to be made well.

Then there is that great host of people for whom we normally write a clean bill of health but who are actually sick and don't know it. We may even recognize ourselves among them. Jesus directed a large part of his healing ministry to the un-sick. In fact, he was speaking sarcastically when he said to the Pharisees, "Those who are well have no need of a physician, but those who are sick," because he obviously considered the Pharisees to be far from well. To his diagnostic mind sickness included not only blindness, paralysis, and insanity; it included lust, hatred, prejudice, vindictiveness, and all those ailments of the spirit that denied men freedom and fullness of life. In his idiom, health denotes wholeness of personality, the perfect integration of all the divergent trends in our bodily, mental, and spiritual life—a blessed state that not many of us enjoy. We may be of sound body and sane mind, but if we harbor attitudes that make us miserable, stultify our relationships, distort our perspective, and stand between us and God, then we have to cry out in the words of the General Confession, "There is no health in us."

That reduces to absurdity the old charge that the Church is full of hypocrites. *Of course* the Church is full of hypocrites. The Church is the place for them. They are not welcome anywhere else; and if the Church doesn't heal them, nobody will. The malicious man, the bitchy woman, the petty perfectionist, who poison the air with misery, are sick people who can never be made well except by a complete change of character which they have not the power within themselves to effect.

The marvelous redemptive organization, Alcoholics Anonymous, tells the compulsive drinker that he has no hope of being cured until he admits his own helplessness, throws himself on the power of God and accepts the support of a caring, healing fellowship of other alcoholics. That is a figure of what the Church ought to be—a caring, healing fellowship of Christians where sin-sick men and women, confessing their helplessness before God, can be cured of their moral sickness and made completely well by the redemptive power of Jesus Christ.

[105

"In obedience to Christ, the Church must be truthful;
it must tell people what he told them,
teach them what he taught,
say what he said,
no more and no less. . . .
Jesus told people that it matters what you believe."

TO TELL THE TRUTH

Chapter 7

We have this ministry ...

To Tell the Truth

ON THE Thames Embankment in London, England, there is a lovely little park that contains a statue of Robert Raikes who organized the first Sunday school in 1780. During my City Temple years I used to stop by that statue and hold imaginary conversations with it.

"Bob," I would say, "it was great while it lasted, but the movement you started is dying. In some places it's already dead."

In my own mind I heard him reply with some indignation, "Then you had better resurrect it, or else find a substitute, because there's no way you can perpetuate the Christian Faith unless you teach it to your children and grandchildren."

There is no other way that the Church can share and

continue the gospel ministry of Jesus. Exploring that ministry as a pattern of what the Church ought to be doing in the world today, we find that we have a representative role; we are to stand between God and man, bringing God into the experience of men and bringing men into the presence of God. Persons must be our priority— not people, principles, or programs, but persons. We must serve persons on their ground, in their needs, at their convenience and not expect to be thanked for it. We must nurture and enable our own members to exercise that servant ministry out in the world, a ministry which can be defined in terms of outreach, evangelism, mission, and healing.

We have yet to explore the most obvious feature of the Gospel ministry of Jesus, the one pointed out by Robert Raikes. It was a teaching ministry. The Gospels portray Jesus primarily as a teacher, and they devote the main bulk of their contents to what he taught. Those who knew Jesus in the days of his flesh would remember him as a rabbi who went from place to place teaching lessons about God and the good life and the coming Kingdom of God. They would remember that he taught ordinary people by means of parables—short stories with a meaning; and also that he had his pupils whom he instructed in brief, pithy sentences which he repeated over and over again and had them recite with him until they could remember them and in time write them down. Jesus consciously cast himself in the role of a teacher. He rejected the more spectacular roles that others would have chosen for him as the promised Messiah. He refused to coerce people or dazzle them or bribe them into the Kingdom of God because he knew that in the long run the human heart can be brought to God only by patient teaching.

Jesus committed a teaching ministry to the Church.

After calling and enabling his first disciples "he sent them out to preach the kingdom of God and to heal" (Luke 9:2). After he rose from the dead he broadened the commission: "Go therefore and make disciples of all nations . . . teaching them to observe all that I have commanded you . . ." (Matt. 28:19–20). If the Church obeys Christ it will indeed be concerned for the Christian education of its children. It will also stress the centrality of preaching—which seemed axiomatic until a few nonpreachers began derogating the sermon as a means of communicating the gospel. The Church will recognize that the primary purpose of outreach at home and abroad is to teach. In a secular society it takes more courage to speak for Christ than to act for Christ, yet we must speak for Christ through every medium and with every technique at our disposal if we seriously hope to exercise the ministry which he has committed to us.

Moreover, Jesus committed a particular teaching to the Church, and he did not expect the Church to confuse that teaching with its own ideas. To be sure, the Church must always be ready to recast the teachings of Jesus in modern thought-forms and reinterpret them to suit the needs of the age; but the Church is not free to tamper with the teachings of Jesus, to add to them or subtract from them in order to suit the spirit of the age. That would be a form of perjury, and the modern pagan has only to read the New Testament for himself in order to see through it. In obedience to Christ, the Church must be truthful; it must tell people what he told them, teach what he taught, say what he said, no more and no less.

THEOLOGY

Jesus told people that it matters what you believe. He

[111

may not have said it in so many words, but neither did he ever say that it does *not* matter what you believe. That big lie is being circulated by latter-day liberals who are anxiously trying to marry the gospel to the spirit of the age, ignorant of the warning that whoever marries the spirit of the age will soon find himself a widower.

The musical revue *Beyond the Fringe* did not spare the Church in its amusing burlesque of British institutions. In one scene a Church of England vicar, not wearing a clerical collar, tries to ingratiate himself with a worldly pair. "You don't have to believe all that God stuff," he says. "No one believes it any more." As they edge away from him, he snuggles closer and tries the man-to-man approach. "Don't call me Vicar. Call me Dick." One of them stammers, "If you say so, Dicker." They are plainly embarrassed by his chummy approach, and everything within them seems to be crying out, "Don't try to win us that way. At least allow us to respect you and what you stand for. If you know something that we don't know, if you believe something that we ought to believe, for heaven's sake be honest and tell us what it is."

There is no doubt that a credibility gap exists today between the Church's Faith (capital F) and the personal faith (small f) of ordinary folk both outside and inside the Church. In its teaching the Church is naturally tempted to bridge the gap by diluting the content of the faith in such a way as to make it acceptable to modern man. To the bewildered believer or the die-hard doubter the Church may be saying, in effect, "You mustn't take the historic Creeds literally. Nobody does any more. Just listen to our new interpretation of them. You will find them much more credible." Yet, as David Read has written in one of his books, "There are surely limits to what can honestly be done to bring the Faith within the reach of every skeptical mind." Dr. Read believes that those limits are now being passed. He says, "The so-called radical theologians of today are not simply restating historic convictions in modern terms. They are gradually eliminating every belief that the world has known as distinctively Christian since Pentecost." [1]

Worse still, the diluters of the Faith have a habit of pointing to Jesus as their authority. They quickly remind us that Jesus simply summoned people to his way of life; he did not demand that they subscribe to formal statements of belief. Perhaps not, but he himself believed certain things. He believed them implicitly, took them for granted and based his way of life on the supposition that they were true. Jesus believed in a living, personal God who knows and sees and loves and helps us, a God so alive and personal that we can pray to him and call him by the name "Father." Jesus believed in the reality of evil, not as a defect in human personality but as an objective force that attacks a man from the outside and throws his world into chaos. Jesus believed that he was the Incarnate Son of God; that the purpose of his life and the purpose of his death was to save men from the power of evil and reconcile them to God. Jesus believed in the Kingdom of God, the final defeat of evil and the triumph of God's righteous rule in human hearts and society, for which we must work within history and which God himself will establish perfectly at the end of history. Jesus believed that death would not be the end of him or of those who identify themselves with him. There are other rooms in the Father's house. "If it were not so," he said, "I would have told you" (John 14:2).

1. David H. C. Read, *Virginia Woolf Meets Charlie Brown* (Grand Rapids: Wm. B. Eerdmans, 1968), p. 206.

[113

Such a guileless thing to say, so completely candid, honest and frank: "If it were not so, I would have told you"! Yet Jesus could say it to his disciples because he had leveled with them from the beginning; he had never lied to them, never spoken anything but the truth. Therefore they could trust him, as men could trust the Church, if the Church were clear in its own mind and made it clear to the world that the gospel of Jesus Christ means some things and not others. If the Church hopes to have the confidence of people as it continues the teaching ministry of Jesus it must be candid, frank and honest as he was; it must tell them the truth, and that means telling them that it does matter what they believe.

MORALITY

Jesus told people that we don't make our own moral ground rules. Another of the big lies being circulated today is that the religion of Jesus contains no rules to regulate human behavior. On the 450th anniversary of the nailing by Martin Luther of the 95 Theses to the church door in Wittenberg a British periodical, *The New Christian* (which has since merged with the *Christian Century*) published its own 95 theses (Oct. 19, 1967) presumably to bring the Reformation up to date. One of them said, "The significance of the ministry of Jesus is to be seen in his unwillingness to provide his followers with a body of doctrine or a code of ethics." That was an astonishing interpretation of the gospel ministry of Jesus.

The Church is not telling the truth when it speaks of the unwillingness of Jesus to provide his followers with a code of ethics. To be sure, Jesus did not start from square one and promulgate a set of rudimentary rules applicable to every form of human behavior, but why should he have to start at square one? The people whom he taught were not ethical kindergarten pupils. They were far advanced in their moral education; they had been well schooled in the moral heritage of the human race, the lessons of purity, decency, honesty, and kindness which wise men had learned by experience and handed down from one generation to another. Jesus took that heritage for granted. He reverenced the Ten Commandments and counseled his followers to make them their starting-point in the Christian life.

But only their starting-point. To the moral rules by which civilized men lived Jesus added a few of his own. What shall we call the Sermon on the Mount but the ethical charter of the Kingdom of God (Matt. 5–7)? He is saying, in effect, "You call yourself good, but what you call good is not enough. You have decided that it is illegal to kill. Well, you can take notice that every time you call another man a fool, your anger has killed him in your heart. You have agreed that adultery is wrong. I tell you that before the face of God one glance of lust is as damnable as any act of lust. You consider it moral to return injury for injury. I tell you that offering the other cheek to him who slaps you is the only moral way to settle a quarrel. You think it human to love your friends. So do thieves and pagans. If you want to be Divine, turn some of your love on your enemies, trade the world your blessing for its curses, help the very man who hates you." Are those not moral rules? Do they not set up an eternal standard of right and wrong that makes our relativism look rather sick?

In the Manned Spacecraft Center at Houston, Texas, I saw an astronaut walking on the wall. Suspended by wires at an 18-degree angle, he was training for survival on a planet where his body would be governed by only

7/10ths of the earth's gravity. The very existence and dependability of such natural laws as the law of gravity make possible the exploration of outer space. We did not create those laws. We believe that they were created by God and we know that we have to live within them if we want to survive in God's world. Is it not possible that a wise, loving, personal God has also created ground rules for the well-being of his human children on earth and that we must live within *them* if we want to survive in God's world? Is it not possible also that he promulgated some of those moral rules through Jesus who was the wisdom and love of God made visible and actual in our experience? That's what Jesus taught and that's what the Church must teach if it hopes to share his continuing ministry.

JUDGMENT

Jesus told people that the gospel of God's grace is also a gospel of judgment. Assuredly the Church has a gospel of grace to proclaim. Our Lord's great trilogy of parables —the lost sheep, the lost coin and the lost son (Luke 15)— authorize us to declare that our God is a gracious God who is sorry for us when we break his ground rules and who freely forgives us when we are sorry and renew our obedience to him. Not only so, but our God takes the initiative, comes where we are, finds us in our disobedience, appeals to us with his love, and graciously reconciles us to himself. Jesus taught and incarnated the gospel of God's grace; and that will always be the Church's first word as it continues the teaching ministry of Jesus.

The Church does not tell the whole truth, however, if it ignores those large areas of Jesus' teaching that communicate a gospel of judgment. Judgment *is* a gospel because it means that God still cares for us and deals with us even in our sin. Over against the parables that speak of God's love and forgiveness we have to set the many parables that portray God as a Judge who not only ordains moral laws but administers those laws and prescribes penalties for people who violate them. Over against the graciousness of Jesus himself we have to set his smashing exposé of the subtle hypocrisies of men's private, corporate, and religious lives and his pronouncement of doom upon them if they persisted in their hypocrisy. Those teachings also he committed to his Church.

Suppose the Church takes those teachings seriously enough to rephrase them in modern idiom and apply them to men's private, corporate, and religious lives today? Look specifically at three of our Lord's parables: first, the parable of the rich fool (Luke 12:16–21). In urban society the farmer would appear as an astute businessman who works hard, makes sound investments, and looks forward to an early retirement. In his affluence he may own a farm in the country as well as a house in the city, but he doesn't worry about building bigger barns to store bigger crops; he worries about bigger dividends to build bigger properties to store the bigger playthings of his increased leisure time. Comes the day when he breathes a sigh of relief and says to his wife, "My dear, at last we can relax. I'm a success. I think we've got it made." Who speaks to him for God? Who dares to say, "Actually you are a fool. One of these nights you're going to have a fatal heart attack. And all this money and property, all these houses and adult toys—what good will they be to you then? Who gets them after you are gone?"

There is the parable of the last judgment at the end of history (Matt. 25:31–46) which ought not to be too difficult to imagine in the light of Paul Ehrlich's book, *The*

[117

Population Bomb.[2] All the people of all the ages stand before Christ who separates them as a shepherd separates the sheep from the goats. He calls the sheep "blessed of my Father," says some nice things about them, and ushers them into his everlasting kingdom. Then he turns to the goats, calls them "cursed," and tells them to go to hell. Why? He gives the reason: "I was hungry and you gave me no food, I was thirsty and you gave me no drink, I was a stranger and you did not welcome me, naked and you did not clothe me, sick and in prison and you did not visit me." The goats are bowled over by the accusation and they protest, "Lord, when did we see thee hungry or thirsty or a stranger or naked or sick or in prison, and did not minister to thee?" So who speaks for Christ today? Who tells the goats in modern society that we really don't have any choice about clearing up the atmosphere and building better houses for the poor and giving them a living wage and stopping wars and equalizing the food supply on the earth's surface, because our eternal destiny depends upon it?

There is the parable of the big banquet (Luke 14:15–24) which in our idiom could be a service of Holy Communion. Christ is the Host who invites us to his Table. As the date draws near, visitors go to the homes of the invited guests with a personal invitation, "Come this Sunday, for all is now ready." Some are courteous enough to admit the visitors but they make excuses, and their excuses are substantially the same as those specified in the New Testament: "We are going to try out the new snowmobile on Sunday . . . We have brought some work home from the office . . . We are entertaining family friends . . . I pray you, have me excused." Christ feels insulted by the

2. Ballantine Books, New York, 1968.

affront. "All right," he explodes. "We don't need them! We'll have a party without them! Go to the ghettos, the slums, the skid-rows, the hospitals, the prisons, the rice fields, the jungles; go to the poor, the dispossessed, the rejected members of society and compel them to come in. Every place at my Table must be filled—if not by the classes, then by the masses; if not by the Church, then by some secular movement that I shall gather in and baptize with forgiving grace and use for my own glad purposes. And as for those spiritual boors who treated my Table with contempt—let them stay away! Don't even admit them if they come!"

Those are not comfortable teachings. They will not raise the Church's stock in society. The Church could even be crucified, as Jesus was crucified, for telling people that the gospel of God's grace is also a gospel of judgment. Crucifixion might bring the Church very close to sharing the gospel ministry of Jesus.

DISCIPLESHIP

Jesus told people that it costs something to be a Christian. He said, "For the gate is narrow and the way is hard, that leads to life, and those who find it are few" (Matt. 7:14). Jesus never portrayed the Christian life as a smooth highway of spiritual tranquillity but always as a rough, rocky, narrow, winding road that will bruise the body and soul of any man who tries to travel it. And he always gave fair warning. Once he said, in effect, "You sit down and count the cost before starting to build a house made with hands. Well, you had better sit down and count the cost before starting to build a house not made with hands" (Luke 14:28–30).

That's why his disciples could trust him so implicitly in

[119

the Upper Room when he held out the hope of heaven and said to them, "If it were not so, I would have told you." He had never lied to them, never told them anything but the truth. From the very day when he called them into his service he had been completely candid, perfectly frank, transparently honest with them about the conditions, the cost, and the rewards of their discipleship. He had come to set them at enmity with their own families and he told them so (Luke 12:51–53). He was sending them out as sheep in the midst of wolves and he told them so (Matt. 10:16). They would be hated by men for the sake of his name, and he told them so (Matt. 10:22). They might have to mutilate their own bodies to get into the Kingdom of God, and he told them so (Mark 9:43–48). They must lose their lives in order to save them, and he told them so (Mark 8:35). If they wanted to follow him they must deny themselves and walk the way of the cross, and he told them so (Mark 8:34). Jesus never hid his scars to win a disciple.

Jesus would rather lose a disciple than win him under false pretenses. That's why he turned many prospective disciples away. There were the three men on the road to Jerusalem who offered to follow him with strings attached; they would join him but on their own terms. Jesus rejected them because he saw that, despite their immediate enthusiasm, they were not prepared to pay the price of Christian obedience (Luke 9:57–62). There was the rich young ruler, a potentially superb disciple whom Jesus instinctively loved but let go, because the young man would not give his material wealth to the poor (Mark 10:17–31). That's not how the church handles an affluent candidate for membership. Never be so tactless as to ask him outright for a sizeable chunk of his money! Get him inside the church first, make him a member of the board, put him on the finance committee, and hope that he will see the need and take the hint. That is how *we* go about winning disciples for Christ. We hoodwink them; we pretend Christianity to be what it is not—a comfortable and pleasant way of life that offers everything and costs nothing, a Christianity minus the cross.

Maybe our dishonesty has caught up with us. Dietrich Bonhoeffer believed so. In his book, *The Cost of Discipleship*, he declared that the deadliest enemy of the Church today is "cheap grace" which he defined as follows:

Cheap grace means grace sold on the market like cheap-jack's wares. The sacraments, the forgiveness of sins, the consolations of religion are thrown away at cut prices. Grace is represented as the Church's inexhaustible treasury from which she showers blessings with generous hands, without asking questions or fixing limits. Grace without price, grace without cost.

Bonhoeffer believed that "cheap grace" more than anything else today has denatured the Church and made it an object of scorn. "This cheap grace has turned on us like a boomerang," he says. "The price we are having to pay in the shape of the collapse of the organized Church is only the inevitable consequence of our policy of making grace available at all too low a cost." [3]

In 1895 George Bernard Shaw, as a benevolent unbeliever, proposed to write his "gospel of Shawianity." Dictating his own terms, he asked, "Where in this world is there a church that will receive me on such terms or into which I could honestly consent to be received?" We don't know what Shaw's terms *were* but we do know what

3. Dietrich Bonhoeffer, *The Cost of Discipleship* (New York: The Macmillan Company, 1961), pp. 35, 45.

Christ's terms *are*. He told people that it matters what you believe, that we don't make our own moral ground rules, that the gospel of God's grace is a gospel of judgment, and that it costs something to be a Christian. Those will be the Church's terms if it tells the truth to men and continues the teaching ministry of Jesus.